Dom Pérignon Vintage 1998

The Collection

© Moët-Hennessy UK 2005

ISBN 1 904122 10 8

CREDITS

Editor and art director: Hervé Landry
Head coach: Mark Harvey
Assistant coach: Alex Field
Chief writer: Lucia van der Post
Technical coordinator: Kirstin Stanley Hughes and Shoshana Silberstein
Assistant technical coordinator: Carmel Perrott
Translator: Christopher Killmartin
Literary consultant and rewriter: Malcolm Scott
Designer: Régis Le Bras
Artist: Sophie von Hellermann
Food photographer: Yutaka Yamamoto
Food stylist: Isabelle Dupuy-Chavanat
Illustrator: Stéphane Gamain
Writer: Cécile Guilbert
Artwork and pre-press: Mark Dawson
Publisher: Ptarmigan Publishing Ltd, Devizes, England
Printer: Butler & Tanner Ltd, London and Frome, England

CONTENTS

photograph overleaf by Karl Lagerfeld

A PERFECT MARRIAGE

There is a famous picture of a pipe by the Belgian surrealist artist René Magritte with the inscription 'ceci n'est pas une pipe' in bold flowing script under the image. In a similar vein, one might inscribe the cover of this book with the proclamation that this is not in fact a book but a great work of art. Whilst consisting physically of no more than bound sheets of high quality paper, this volume has been transformed by superb craftsmanship and artistic flair into an objet d'art of transcendent opulence and magnificence. It celebrates the unforgettable encounter between an exceptional vintage – Dom Pérignon 1998 – and matchless culinary creativity.

On these pages recipes and images have been woven into a rich counterpoint, like the musical scores on which great operas and symphonies depend. They constitute a glowing chronicle with which to immortalise, even recreate (for the gifted and the brave!), the subtle resonances and exquisite harmonies that thirty five peerless gastronomic creations and a superb vintage champagne have engendered.

Though every cuvée of Dom Pérignon is, by definition, exceptional, the 1998 vintage is extraordinary in many ways - not the least of which is its survival of extreme climatic conditions. In August of that year, record temperatures led to fires in the fields of Hautvilliers, followed by exceptionally high rainfalls in September. The grapes that emerged were magnificently succulent and pulpy – qualities that have translated directly into the wine itself. On the nose, the initial salvo of sweet almonds, impregnated by hints of grapefruit, is relayed by the spicy aroma of cashew nuts and finishes with delightful notes of lightly toasted brioche. The dominant sensation on the palate is that of a long, creamy wave of silk, the endless caress of which is a hallmark of the seamless perfection that Dom Pérignon can achieve. That silkiness persists in the mouth with infinitely subtle modulations before finally fading away to the accompaniment of zests of citrus. The magnetic, vibrating radiance of Dom Pérignon 1998 will bewitch the senses, and subtly deploy a wealth of seductive charms.

Because each vintage is a celebration of the creative synergy between man and nature, Dom Pérignon has decided to pay homage to those chefs whose vocation it is to transform natural ingredients by means of their creativity and talent. In return thirty five chefs, in charge of the most prestigious and well-appointed kitchens in the United Kingdom, have paid homage to Dom Pérignon and revealed some of the secrets of their art in a series of hedonistic epiphanies.

Thus 'Dom Pérignon Vintage 1998 The Collection' was born. As carefully conceived, as preciously crafted as a medieval missal or book of hours, a special edition has been created that has the extravagant disregard for expense that is the mark of true luxury – 'qui aime ne compte pas'. Bound in dark sea-green galuchat (rayskin), it evokes one of Chardin's mouth-wateringly sensuous still lives. Its structure is dominated by the figures seven and five, numerological symbols of wholeness and perfection the world over. It is divided into seven chapters that define the seven hallmarks of excellence of the Dom Pérignon 1998 vintage – and each chapter contains five recipes, one from each of our esteemed thirty five chefs. All of which is accompanied by commentaries from eminent figureheads of the international cultural scene.

Anxious that the artistic quality should be no less sumptuous than the text of this precious tome, Dom Pérignon has commissioned three major contemporary artists to illustrate our artistic endeavour.

Sophie von Hellermann, portraitist of Mick Jagger, has contributed a series of entertaining, witty vignettes of high life amongst the 'glitterati', while the thirty five portraits of the contributing chefs by Stéphane Gamain combine classical mastery with state-of-the-art digital technology in a subtle, stylistic exercise that echoes the early twentieth century woodcuts of Félix Valloton.

Lastly, the Japanese photographer Yutaka Yamamoto has produced exquisitely decorative yet minimalist still lives that are of a refined elegance as fluid and heady as a glass of Dom Pérignon.

Given its legendary status as the hallmark of glamour, it would be remiss of Dom Pérignon not to pay homage to outstanding personalities in the worlds of commerce, arts and entertainment. As Truman Capote with Elizabeth Taylor in a previous age, the scintillating Lucia van der Post conducts a series of interviews over a glass of champagne with Theo Fennell, Joanne Harris, Philip Green, Sir Roger Moore, Meredith Etherington-Smith, and Lord Lloyd Webber, who recount their gastronomico-bibulous adventures taking the mythic marriage of Dom Pérignon and British haute cuisine as their inspiration.

This illustrious cohort is the counterpart in print of an equally glamorous gathering that met in June last year at a reception in New York for the launch of the Dom Pérignon 1998 vintage. The culmination of a campaign magisterially orchestrated by the incomparable Karl Lagerfeld (featuring photographs that unveiled his muse Helena Christensen, the archetype of elegant sensuality, in a series of provocative tableaux vivants), that reception was the precursor to this volume. But the Dom Pérignon 1998 Vintage Collection is more than a mere souvenir: it is both the concentrated essence of that event, as well as a tribute to the creative, visionary spirit of a humble seventeenth century monk called Dom Pérignon. It was Dom Pérignon who first undertook the voyage into the world of aromas, textures and taste - a sensuous odyssey that has culminated ultimately in the mythic marriage of Dom Pérignon and British gastronomy in this book.

Long may the delectable virtues of its issue, 'Dom Pérignon Vintage 1998 The Collection', regale the spirits and the senses of gastronomes and connoisseurs the world over!

RICHARD GEOFFROY
Chef de Cave, Dom Pérignon

"If life gives you lemons, make some kind of fruity juice."

CONAN O'BRIEN

Joanne Harris
by Sophie von Hellermann

Fruiti

ness

The golden grapes of Dom Pérignon Vintage 1998 release a bouquet laden with the rich vibrations of their liquescent pulp. After a fruity attack redolent of sweet almonds, soon penetrated by tart, fleshy hints of grapefruit, this palette of blossoming aromas, sublimated by a halo of spices tinged with the scent of cashew nuts, is accompanied in a discreet descant by the buttery suggestion of toasted brioche.

Fruitiness

Jean-Christophe Novelli

AUBERGE DU LAC

Jean-Christophe Novelli grew up in Arras, Northern France, and first became interested in food by watching his mother cook. Though they were poor she would make meals such as mince-stuffed tomatoes glazed with Beaufort cheese and thyme flowers that remain among Novelli's favourite dishes today. Even with all his experience he still doesn't think he can make them half as well as his mother.

He began his working life as a slightly unruly 14 year old, helping to clean the bread tins in a bakery. Despite this less than glamorous introduction to catering, he soon became hooked on kitchens and cooking, moving on to a brasserie where he claims he used to make 'the quickest omelette on the block'. Following National Service (which he hated) Novelli found himself working in a hotel in Corsica. Although the island introduced him to the charms of fresh seafood – particularly lobsters, sea bass and crab – arguably the most significant factor in this period of his development was that the hotel was owned by the Rothschilds, and it was Elie Rothschild who persuaded him he ought to try life in England.

Shortly after crossing la Manche, Novelli's life began to look up. He started cooking in Southampton where he was discovered by the restaurant critic Jonathan Meades. The latter introduced him to Marco Pierre White, and he went on to meet Rick Stein, Keith Floyd and other luminaries of the British culinary world. He won his first Michelin star at Provence, a restaurant in Hampshire, and has followed it up with several more since.

His culinary ability has never been in question, and his work with classic French dishes such as pig's trotters and grilled scallops at Auberge du Lac in the grounds of Brocket Hall, a beautiful Hertfordshire country house, has turned it into a real destination restaurant. He loves socialising around food and thinks that people are beginning to turn away from uncivilised notions such as 'grazing' all day and beginning, instead, to realise that eating together is a civilising, pleasure-giving activity. As, indeed, is champagne.

Novelli remembers the first time he drank champagne very well – it was at his cousin's Holy Communion and he was just eight years old. He sneaked into the kitchen, ate the food, drank the champagne and was later discovered in the wine cellar.

The basis of his cooking is a passionate belief that getting it right matters. But though he cooks in the classical French tradition he also believes in being creative, in finding new tastes and textures that work together. Novelli's own tastes in food can be heavily influenced by whether or not he's training for events such as the London Triathlon, which necessitate his consuming lots of pasta and fresh fruit for the carbohydrates and vitamin C. Surprisingly for a chef he isn't fond of cooking onions and he doesn't like drinking Noilly Prat – though he's perfectly happy to use it in his cooking.

Andalouse of sole

Sole
6 large sole fillets
1 vanilla pod
thyme flower
bay leaves

Piperade
6 warm soft-boiled eggs, halved
400ml olive oil
1 large courgette, sliced at an angle
2 medium aubergines, sliced at an angle, then halved
8 large shallots, peeled
8 baby fennel, trimmed
2 red peppers, de-seeded & cut in half
2 yellow peppers, de-seeded & cut in half
2 green peppers, de-seeded & cut in half
1 head of garlic, cloves separated & peeled
3 star anise
freshly ground salt & pepper
good handful of black olives
a carton of sun-dried tomato juice reduced to one-third
20 basil leaves
handful of mixed fresh herbs, to serve
200g sun-dried tomatoes
10 red cherry tomatoes
200ml truffle oil
sugar

Garnish
Parmesan
rocket, mizuna – hold in cold water

To prepare the piperade, heat the olive oil in a pan,
add the vegetables, garlic and sun-dried tomato juice and season.
Cover the pan with a tight-fitting lid and leave over a low heat
until the vegetables are just soft to the touch.
Remove the vegetables from the heat
and add the olives and basil to warm through.
Carefully arrange the vegetables on the plates with the soft-boiled eggs.

To prepare the sole fillets, brush them with a little olive oil
and vanilla seed and season. Grill for about 2-3 minutes on each side,
skin side upwards first. If the fillets are quite thick,
they may require a further minute on each side.
Place a sole fillet on each dish with the vegetables.
Add fresh herbs and Parmesan to garnish.

Martyn Nail

Claridge's

Gordon Ramsay might be the best-known name at Claridge's with his eponymous restaurant, but Martyn Nail, as the Executive Chef for the rest of the hotel, is the one whose food is most often ordered. His interest in food was fired slowly, in time-honoured way, by watching his grandmother cook the dishes and recipes that her grandmother had probably cooked before her. He remembers the plum jam she made every year, the puddings and the roasts, evocative traditional homely dishes that children love and adults never really grow out of.

Nail is proud of the fact that he's only ever had one McDonald's in his life, because that sort of food gives him no pleasure at all. He'd rather have something truly simple, a plate of salad, say, than something that he can't recognise and doesn't understand.

For a chef (usually an adventurous breed) he is rather reserved. He doesn't much like going anywhere unknown and cites an episode in Belgrade as being his worst food nightmare. It was bad enough that he didn't know exactly what the food was, and the fact that it was so badly cooked made it a truly awful experience.

Rather more pleasurable was his first taste of champagne, which came when he was 11. He'd just won a race riding a friend's horse and a bottle of Dom Pérignon was cracked open to celebrate. This was doubly fitting since not only was it his mother's favourite champagne, it was also the name of the horse!

Perhaps it was here that Nail first had the inklings of the palate that was to turn him into a top chef. Despite having his young brain somewhat addled by the champagne, he remembers how when he drank it with a lemon posset the two combined to give a really zesty, citrussy flavour. He certainly thinks it's a better combination than red wine and mint, which he can't abide – something of a problem given this country's attachment to mint sauce with its lamb. Nor is he keen on 'eating things which had a purpose' such as offal.

Key to Nail's food philosophy is the idea that food can be appreciated at many different levels, and that it's up to the chef to recognise this. He sees little point in trying to push esoteric or strongly flavoured dishes if they're not likely to be enjoyed by the diners, however much he personally would like to cook them. 'It's important to try and understand what would give your friends or customers real pleasure,' he says reasonably. 'As a chef you're cooking for them, not for yourself.' This is particularly true in a hotel (which has to cater to a wide range of people) rather than a restaurant, which diners have usually sought out specifically and where it's easier for a chef to put his personality on display.

At home the food is usually simple, as you might expect for this self-effacing man – perhaps some steak, salad and a few potatoes, though his love of Mediterranean food means there's usually a tomato and basil salad lurking in the background.

A progressive tasting of hand dived scallop ceviche

PER SERVING

1 scallop large enough
for 4 good slices

Pineapple water	First marinade	Second marinade	Third marinade	Fourth marinade
1 pineapple skin	red onion	diced tomato	spring onion	coconut milk
water	coriander	1 chilli	orange zest	
2 chillies	lemon juice	basil	ginger	
		mint	wasabi soy sauce	
		lemon oil		
		olive oil		

Pineapple water
Remove the skin from a pineapple,
cover the skin with water and add the chillies. Leave for 2 days.

First marinade
Dice the ingredients, then mix with the pineapple water.
Spoon this marinade over the top of the first sliced scallop.

Second marinade
Dice the ingredients, then mix with the first marinade.
Spoon the new marinade over the top of the second sliced scallop.

Third marinade
Dice, then mix with the second marinade.
Spoon the new marinade over the top of the third sliced scallop.

Fourth marinade
Finally, take a spoonful of the third marinade,
add it to coconut milk, and spoon over the fourth sliced scallop.

Philip Leach

COMBE HOUSE HOTEL

Philip Leach is a big believer in the quality of a dish's raw materials doing the talking. He has never been a fan of fussy food, preferring instead that a dish bring out the natural flavours and textures of its ingredients. As you might expect, he's dedicated to using local produce, and was delighted when his commitment was recognised by an award for the best use of local west country food in Devon Life Magazine, which also gave Combe House Hotel its coveted Best Restaurant award.

This award wasn't the first one he'd picked up. When he was a boy, growing up in Rustington, Sussex, he used to watch his sister win the village's cookery competition year after year. His culinary ambitions (not to mention sibling rivalry) were aroused, and the very first year he entered he won the cup. He was 7 at the time.

He was quite old when he first tasted champagne, at Manley's restaurant in Sussex. It was the New Year's Eve of 1990, the champagne was Moët & Chandon, and he was 20. It was also at Manley's, where he worked for a while, that he learned how enriching it could be to find a great food and wine match – something that the chef there was very passionate about.

At home he cooks mostly rather traditional foods: risottos, fresh breads, stews, hot pots and so on. As life gets busier and more stressful he thinks it is increasingly important for friends and family to take time to eat together, to sit down over good food and good wine and chew the fat. But preferably not over very heavy red wines or plates of tripe, both of which he dislikes.

Salmon gravlax

1 x 8-10lb organic salmon gutted, filleted, trimmed & pin boned
4 tablespoons black peppercorns
half a cup firmly packed light soft brown sugar
half a cup coarse sea salt
one and a half cups finely chopped mixed dill & parsley
half a cup brandy

Blend the peppercorns, sugar and salt in a blender to a smooth paste.

Place the salmon fillets on a tray skin side down and spread first the paste,
then a layer of chopped herbs over both fillets. Pour the brandy over the fillets,
then tightly wrap them both in cloth.
Place the wrapped fish on a rack under a heavily weighted tray.

Turn the fillets every 24 hours. The recipe will take two or sometimes three days,
after which the flesh should feel firm to the touch.
When ready wash off excess herbs and pat the fillets dry.
Slice from the tail end, cutting very thinly:
you should be able to see newsprint through the slices.

Serve with a quenelle of dill crème fraîche and some dressed leaves.

Jamie Forman

THE COTSWOLD HOUSE HOTEL

Family holidays in Cornwall (specifically a small restaurant in Newlyn called Smugglers) might have started Jamie Forman's love for food, but it wasn't until much later, following time working in Canada and travelling in France, that he really began to understand what the culinary arts were all about.

France, as well as being where he first tasted champagne, gave him an appreciation of the heritage and cultural roots of cuisine, while in Canada and the USA he saw that food was a way of entertaining people and bringing them together. Perhaps not unrelated to the idea of mealtimes as a social occasion, Forman has a strong understanding of the difference that serving the right wine can make to a dish. His love of wine also began with family holidays, when he and his parents used to travel through Europe in a caravan, stopping off at small wineries en route and tasting the samples on offer. This embryonic appreciation really blossomed once he began to cook professionally, and he cites a particularly good match of venison and Rioja as the moment when he fully began to understand just how good a first class food and wine combination could be.

His approach to cooking is straightforward. He believes in taking the best seasonal ingredients and finding ways of serving them that show them to their full advantage. It's simple food with a contemporary twist, classical techniques with modern touches.

At home he makes simple salads, often with his own home-grown mustard cress and radishes, but he is also a big fan of the archetypal lavish Sunday roast which he likes to share with friends and family, ideally with lashings of wine.

There's just about nothing that he himself won't eat or drink, but he admits to being a stickler for quality, whether in food or wine. 'I hate the headaches that cheap plonk gives you,' he says.

Ballotine of foie gras with Dom Pérignon 1998 jelly

SERVES 8-10

Ballotine
500g grade A foie gras
2 teaspoons salt
3 twists white pepper
half a teaspoon sugar
1 teaspoon pink salt
sprinkle of white port
200ml veal stock

Jelly
170g sugar
170ml water
two and a half leaves gelatine
150ml Dom Pérignon 1998
50g diced champagne grapes

Bring the foie gras to room temperature, de-vein, then press into a flat tray,
season with the ballotine mix and sprinkle with port. Leave to marinate in the fridge overnight,
then remove and trim into shape. Wrap in muslin and poach in stock for 2 minutes,
then refresh in iced water. Wring the ends of the muslin to squeeze out any excess fat and tie with string,
then wrap tightly in a clean cloth and hang in the fridge.

For the jelly, warm the water and Dom Pérignon 1998 and dissolve the sugar in the liquid.
Add and dissolve the soaked gelatine leaves, then add the diced grapes.
Allow to cool, then pour into portion sized moulds to set.

To serve, unwrap the foie gras and slice into portions 4cm thick.
Season with Sel de Guérande and crushed black pepper.
De-mould the jelly and arrange on the plate with the foie gras.

Serving suggestions: toasted brioche or onion bread,
and perhaps a salad of finely cut apple and chervil.

John McManus

ASHDOWN PARK
HOTEL AND COUNTRY CLUB

Ashdown Park is perhaps one of Britain's best-kept secrets, and it's no exaggeration to say that it deserves to be infinitely better known than it is. Credit for its rise up the ratings must go to chef John McManus, who has made a point of concentrating on mainly classic food using only the finest ingredients.

Although at home he tends to make simple food (fish, pasta, risotto), when people come to his restaurant he's keen that they spread their wings and try food that they wouldn't normally eat. He helps them in their journey of discovery by putting new slants on old favourites, or putting together unusual combinations of food.

McManus' own journey of culinary discovery began when he was 14. A lecturer from the local catering college was demonstrating how to flambé crêpe suzettes, and somewhere in amongst the fire and smoke he thought 'I want to be able to do that'.

Like most chefs he believes that good (healthy) food with friends and family is one of the fundamentals for a satisfactory life, particularly if it includes decent wine. McManus, who discovered the joys of champagne at the age of 15, came to the idea of food and wine matching early as well, an interest that was encouraged by his lecturers at catering college.

McManus is passionate about his food and drink, and not slow to point the finger at things he doesn't like. Top of his hit list are processed crab sticks – 'they must be the most disgusting thing on the planet' – the dozens of new 'cholesterol free' butters coming on the market ('why not just eat proper butter but less often?') and home-made wines such as elderberry. It has to be said, he has a point …

Chocolate and vanilla torte

MAKES 10 PORTIONS

400g chocolate Genoese sponge, 5 mm thick

Vanilla mousse
300ml cream
2 vanilla pods, split with seeds scraped out
4 egg whites
100g sugar
2 leaves gelatine, soaked in cold water

Black velvet ice cream
300ml milk
330ml Guinness, reduced by half
300ml cream
190ml Dom Pérignon '98 champagne
2 egg yolks
200g sugar

Dom Pérignon '98 Froth
100ml stock syrup (50ml sugar dissolved in 50ml water)
2 egg yolks
100ml Dom Pérignon '98 champagne

For the vanilla mousse, whisk the cream and vanilla seeds.
Make a meringue with the sugar and egg white: dissolve the soaked gelatine in a little warm cream.
Fold the cream mixture into the meringue.
Pass the dissolved gelatine through a fine chinois into the meringue mixture
and continue folding in until thoroughly combined.

Bring the milk and cream for the ice cream to the boil.
Combine and pour the egg yolks and sugar over the boiling milk and cream,
cook out until the mixture coats the back of a spoon, then chill.
Meanwhile reduce both the Guinness and 90ml of the champagne by half,
and add them to the ice cream mix once it has chilled.
Churn the mixture in the ice-cream machine:
when half churned add the rest of the champagne and finish churning.
Store in a suitable container in the freezer.

Place all the ingredients for the Dom Pérignon '98 froth
in a round based bowl and whisk over a bain-marie until light and airy.

To assemble, take ten 60 x 70mm round moulds.
Cut the sponge into rounds with a pastry cutter, allowing 3 discs per portion.
Place the moulds on parchment paper on a baking tray.
Place one disc on the base of the mould and pipe in vanilla mixture until it is approximately half full.
Insert another disc and repeat, finishing with the final disc.

Leave the moulds to set the in the fridge for 4-6 hours,
then turn them out with a warm knife, carefully easing it around the edge.
Place the mousse on serving plate and arrange a scoop of the ice cream next to it.
Carefully spoon the froth around the plate and finish with a sprig of mint or chocolate,
then serve immediately.

"Next year, they always said, we'll have Dom Pérignon. But of course next year never came."

JOANNE HARRIS BY LUCIA VAN DER POST

You would expect a writer whose first three books were entitled 'Chocolat', 'Blackberry Wine' and 'Five Quarters of an Orange' to have a more than passing interest in food, and you'd be right. Joanne Harris might have grown up in England, but her French mother made her aware that food was more than just something to eat to keep you alive; it was a way of keeping a family in touch with its roots. 'Food,' she says now, 'is one of the main aspects of sensuality, and has always interested me'.

Her mother came from a large French family, and they would visit them in Brittany several times a year. Each visit was a cause of much celebration – nearly always accompanied by champagne – with all the women cooking together, singing and telling stories. They always found some small jobs for the children to do so they weren't left out, and some of Harris's earliest memories are of the super-fresh seafood: the mackerel, crabs, oysters and the skate with black butter and capers. Yet just 20 miles inland at her grandmother's, the fruits de mer gave way to charcuterie, sausages and pancakes.

The regionality of the food, she feels, didn't just keep her in touch with her roots, but also with her ancestors. The ancient recipes they'd left behind were still turned to – and eventually passed on – by the current generation.

Harris might have been welcomed into the world with a tiny drop of champagne in her mouth, but because she came from a large family of mainly schoolmasters they weren't able to afford expensive sparklers on a regular basis. 'Next year,' they always said, 'we'll have Dom Pérignon. But of course next year never came.' Not that it was all bad news, since it did, at least, introduce her to the name of Dom Pérignon very early on.

Harris cooks daily herself, the sort of simple food with fresh ingredients that she learned to enjoy from her French mother, and is adamant about never serving anything that comes in a disposable container or a foil tray.

'If I don't have time to cook I'd rather assemble some good cheese and olives, fresh bread and some wine than serve something slushy and indeterminate and filled with chemical stabilisers,' she says.

If she had the chance to choose her last supper on earth it would be accompanied by Dom Pérignon all the way through, with a Château d'Yquem to accompany the dessert. She'd share the meal with her husband Kevin and her daughter Anouchka, and it would take place on the beach at her grandfather's house on the island of Noirmoutier.

She would eat the things she remembers from her childhood: rock crabs simply boiled and served with butter and salt, then a leg of lamb cooked the way her grandmother did it with garlic and rosemary and served with flageolets. After that there would be some of the wonderful goat's cheeses from the region and she'd finish with a Pièce Monte of tiny choux buns, filled with cream, piled upon each other and held together with spun sugar and topped with nuts and honey.

'I used to see them at posh weddings where they looked like wonderful, gleaming pirate's treasure, and I always wanted one. But in the end my mother said it was too much trouble to make and the family would buy something from the pâtisserie.'

"Jenny Lind soup:
stock, sage,
raw eggs,
half pint of cream.
For creamy
dreamy ..."

ULYSSES, JAMES JOYCE

Philip Green
by Sophie von Hellermann

Cream

miness C

The texture, light and fluid, of Dom Pérignon Vintage 1998 unfurls like a pliant wave cradling – half-perceived, ethereal – the undulating folds of the subtlest of taffetas. Slipping slowly, progressively, into ever deeper zones of pleasure, the palate is left with a soft creamy taste by the suavest of kisses, the froth of an embrace.

reaminess

Michael Caines

GIDLEIGH PARK
HOTEL & RESTAURANT

Michael Caines, Head Chef at Gidleigh Park, is one of Britain's youngest two-Michelin-starred chefs. He trained under some of the culinary world's leading lights – Raymond Blanc and Joel Robuchon to name but two – and is noted for his understanding of classical techniques, to which he brings his own particular brand of imagination.

One of six children, there was no room for passengers in the Caines household. His father, a keen gardener, grew the vegetables while his mother cooked the food, and the children were expected to join in if they wanted their pocket money. At an early age Caines realised both that he preferred helping in the kitchen rather than out in the garden, and that mealtimes were an important, almost religious occasion in the way they brought the family together. He's never forgotten that.

As a child, champagne was seen as being out of reach, something only for special occasions unless you were very wealthy. And though he realised that it had an important role in celebration, his real passion for it began when he lived in France, where the drink was less a matter of status and more an intrinsic part of the French way of life as well as, of course, a wonderful apéritif. For Caines, to be interested in food means an inevitable interest in wine – 'it goes with the territory' – and he even goes so far as describing it as 'criminal' not to recognise this.

He won't compromise when it comes to quality of ingredients and he tries to buy locally if he can, partly to give a sense of regional identity to the restaurant and partly to allow for greater traceability – to make sure that every ingredient delivers the flavours it should. At home he prefers not to cook at all (it helps having a wife, Ruth, whom he says is a 'brilliant cook') though if guests come round he will treat them to food similar to that which he cooks at Gidleigh Park.

One thing he's unlikely to cook at home is smoked or farmed salmon (though he loves wild salmon). 'When I was a child smoked salmon was always supposed to be such a treat, but actually it's not expensive these days, and nor is it very nice,' he sighs.

Tartlet of quail and quail eggs with onion confit, summer truffle and smoked bacon, wild mushrooms and a light quail jus

4 quail
16 quail eggs
100g mixed wild mushrooms, diced
spinach

Tartlets
250g plain flour
65g butter
1 egg yolk
60ml water
5g salt
30g sugar

Onion confit
200g button onions, sliced
50g smoked bacon cut into small lardons
100g whipping cream
50g butter

Prepare the tartlet dough at least 4 hours in advance so that it can firm up and lose its elasticity.
Rub the butter and the flour until the mixture resembles fine grains of sand.
Mix the remaining ingredients together and add progressively.
Blend until mixed, then shape into a ball, wrap in cling film and refrigerate.
Roll out the pastry and line four buttered brioche moulds:
refrigerate for 15 minutes before baking, then bake at 160°C for 15-20 minutes.
Leave to cool, then remove the tartlet cases from the moulds.

Onion confit
Slowly cook the sliced onions in a saucepan with the butter and a pinch of salt.
Once they are soft, place them in a sieve to strain off the excess butter.
Pan-fry the lardons without colour in a little oil, then strain off the excess fat.
Mix the onions and lardons together. Reduce the cream by half,
then add it to the onion and lardon mix and season with salt and pepper.

Quail
Roast off the quail in the oven at 200°C for 6 minutes.
Leave to rest for 10 minutes, then take the meat off the bone.

Take the quail eggs and carefully break them into a saucepan with some cold water and a dash of vinegar.
Bring a pan of water with a pinch of salt to the boil then pour in the eggs.
Once cooked, lightly remove the eggs from the water with a slotted spoon and refresh in iced water.
Reheat in a sieve in boiling water when needed.

Cook the spinach and pan fry the diced mushroom in a little butter with salt and pepper.
Place a small amount of spinach in the bottom of each tartlet, followed by the mushroom.
Spoon in onion confit and top with the poached quail eggs.
Reheat the quail meat, arrange on top of the tartlet, and serve.

Daniel Richardson

Hartwell House
Hotel, Restaurant and Spa

Daniel Richardson has been the Head Chef at Hartwell House for around four years now, during which time he's earned all manner of awards. His reputation has been based on his passionate commitment to clean flavours, to using local organic game and meat and only the freshest of herbs and vegetables.

Like Jamie Oliver he worries about the dietary habits of the younger generation, and has embarked on a programme to help them discover the delights of proper food as opposed to the over-salted, grease-laden fare provided by most fast-food outlets. He has banned all junk food for his own children.

There was no Damascene conversion to the cause of good food. He simply found that he enjoyed cooking when he was introduced to it at school, and had always enjoyed eating good food, so went away and studied it. He freely acknowledges the influence that Jamie Oliver had on his thinking – 'I learned so much watching his programmes' – and believes strongly in the fundamental importance of sitting down en famille at the dining table.

He learned quite early on the difference between cheap sparkling wines and real champagne. 'I remember clearly when I was at the Meridien Hotel in Piccadilly and we were offered champagne at the leaving do of one of the chefs. Though I'd only drunk the fake stuff before I could immediately tell the difference,' he says. Although he admits to having sneakily drunk champagne in the larder in the afternoons, he doesn't, as a whole, drink very much, and prefers to let the sommelier choose the wine for him when he's eating out. It is, as he points out, a 'good way to learn'.

Marrying flavours is at the heart of his cooking. He likes to take the freshest, most natural products and cook them simply, the art lying in the skilful mixing of flavours, in contrasting tastes and textures. The food he likes to cook in the restaurant – fresh seafood, fresh meat, plenty of salads – is also the sort he likes to eat at home.

While there are a few foods he doesn't like on their own – anchovies and olives, for instance – he usually finds that there are ways of combining them in dishes which transforms them. The same is true for wines, some of which may not show brilliantly when drunk alone but which come into their own when served up with the right foods.

Paupiette of veal flavoured with shallot and garden herbs, sweetbreads, and Bordelaise potatoes

SERVES 4

Veal paupiette
4 x 180g veal escalopes
50g shallot, finely diced
20g chopped parsley, chervil & chives
5g butter

Sweetbreads
500g veal sweetbreads
50ml chicken stock
two sprigs thyme
500ml milk
80g morels
10ml Madeira
150ml red wine sauce
15g salt

Spring vegetables
25 asparagus tips
600g fresh broad beans
600g fresh peas

Bordelaise potatoes
2kg Pentland Javelin potatoes
100g salted butter
20g parsley, finely chopped
100g garlic infused oil

Prepare the sweetbreads by first soaking them in milk and salt overnight to remove the blood.

Veal paupiette
Sweat down the shallot in the butter, then add the mixed herbs, season, and leave to cool.
Lay the escalopes on cling film, season the veal, then spread thickly with the shallot mixture.
Roll the veal up tightly to form a boudin in the cling film. Place in the fridge.

Sweetbreads
Remove from the milk and wash in running water. Bring the seasoned chicken stock and thyme sprigs to a simmer,
add the sweetbreads and gently poach for 8 minutes, then remove from the heat and leave to cool in the stock.
Once cool remove the white outer membrane and break the sweetbreads into nuggets along the natural seams,
then dry and keep in the fridge.

Spring vegetables
Prepare the asparagus tips, peeling the stalk to approximately 6cm lengths.
Blanch in boiling salted water and refresh in iced water. Keep in the fridge.
Prepare the broad beans and peas separately in the same way:
first depodding then blanching the beans in boiling salted water and refreshing in iced water,
then removing the skin to reveal the green flesh. Store in the fridge.

Bordelaise potatoes
Peel and cut the potatoes to a 2cm dice, allowing 5 pieces per person.
Blanch the potatoes in boiling salted water, then dry and keep in the fridge.

To finish the dish, place the veal in a slow oven at 65°C for 45 minutes, then transfer to a hot pan.
Season and brown in salted foaming butter. Pan fry the potatoes in the garlic oil and butter until golden brown all over,
and finish with the chopped parsley. Lightly dust the sweetbreads in seasoned flour, pan fry until golden brown,
then add the fresh morels and deglaze with the Madeira and 50ml of the red wine sauce.
Warm the peas, broadbeans and asparagus in a little butter, season and keep warm. Warm 100ml of red wine sauce.

To assemble, place 5 potato pieces evenly around the outside of the plate.
Slice the veal at an angle to a 3mm thickness and fan around the plate.
In the centre place the sweetbread and morel fricassée.
Scatter the asparagus, peas and broad beans and finish with a cordon of jus.

Paul Gayler

THE LANESBOROUGH

If your parents run a catering company, you're going to grow up either obsessed or totally uninterested in food. For Paul Gayler, it was the former. His father (a former toastmaster in the city) and mother had started up their own catering business by the time he was 12, and he remembers helping out his mother in the kitchen with what he calls 'simple food'. By the time he was 15 he had moved on to helping his father at his newly-opened Chinese restaurant. This may explain why, as Executive Chef of The Lanesborough for the last ten years, he has given the hotel's cuisine such a distinctive style, blending European traditions with Oriental flavours.

Unsurprisingly, given his foodie upbringing, Gayler is a big fan of the French concept of the lengthy lunch, though he does wonder how they do it since he himself seems scarcely able to get his children (he's got four) to sit down for five minutes.

He first drank champagne as a youngster at weddings, but has drunk plenty of it since. 'Most chefs drink champagne like you or I would water,' he says with a grin. 'As soon as one chef visits another a glass of champagne is poured before you're even offered a cup of tea.'

Gayler is a fan of the whole food and wine-pairing concept. Though he accepts that most chefs are only slowly coming round to the importance of the liquid in the glass as well as the food on the plate, the fact that he now gets asked to devise menus and recommend wines to go with them is proof of how far expectations have changed regarding a chef's wine knowledge. He himself is taking wine much more seriously and is even doing a special course. 'It's embarrassing if people ask you to recommend a wine and you can't help them,' he says. He loves most wines, but favourite of all is Dom Pérignon …

He thinks food should be interesting, stimulating and appealing to the eye, but also that it must cater to customers' tastes. People travel so much more that menus have, inevitably, had to become more cosmopolitan, he thinks, with Thai-style fish as well as risotto on the list.

Gayler doesn't cook much at home, for the simple reason that he's hardly ever there. As a result, his wife does most of the cooking, including the Sunday roast. But when they entertain he's expected to dust off his knives, don his apron and get stuck in. When he does cook at home, he tends to shy away from the rich foods he typically creates at the hotel, preferring something fast and simple – often putting his love of Oriental food to good use with a stir fry.

Gayler has very few foods that he doesn't like: in fact, his big bugbear is a lack of adventur-ousness in others. He gets irritated with people who won't try anything new or declare they don't like something without tasting it. 'If you were to give somebody brains to eat without telling them what it was, they might well love it,' he muses. 'But as soon as you tell them what it is they're shocked. A lot of it's all in the mind.'

Braised veal sweetbreads with morels, truffles, and caramelised apples

SERVES 4

4 x 225g veal sweetbreads
1 fresh (or canned) truffle, thinly sliced
2 carrots, chopped
1 onion, chopped
500ml dry white wine (or, even better, champagne)
500ml veal stock
1 Granny Smith apple, peeled, cored, & cut into wedges
100g fresh morels (or 10g dried morels)
1 tablespoon caster sugar
50g unsalted butter
salt & freshly ground black pepper

Clean the sweetbreads by soaking them in a bowl of cold water for 2 hours to remove any blood traces.
Place in a pan, cover with cold water and bring to the boil, then reduce the heat and cook for 10 minutes.
Remove with a slotted spoon directly into cold water. Trim off the outer nerves, membranes and skin.

In a casserole, heat 20g of the butter, add the sweetbreads and chopped vegetables and lightly cook for 8-10 minutes.
Pour over the wine or champagne, bring to the boil, then cook for 2-3 minutes before adding the veal stock.
Cover with a lid and cook over a low heat for 20 minutes or until the sweetbreads are tender, then remove and keep them warm.

Pass the sauce from the pan through a fine strainer, then return to the heat and add the truffles and morels
and cook for 2-3 minutes. Heat the remaining butter in a frying pan with the sugar,
add the apples and cook over a low heat for 2-3 minutes until they are golden and caramelised.

Slice each sweetbread into 4 slices, top with apple, pour over the finished sauce, and serve.
Fresh leaf spinach and creamy mashed potatoes will go wonderfully with this dish.

Michel Roux Jr

LE GAVROCHE

Michel Roux Jr is a culinary legend and his Le Gavroche, a three-star Michelin for some 20 years, has long been one of the starriest watering holes in London. His culinary antecedents are impeccable in that he was – almost literally – born in a kitchen. His mother and father were working in the kitchens of the Cazalets, trainers of the Queen Mother's horses, when his mother went into labour.

No wonder that the man himself feels that his future life as a chef was practically written in the stars. Certainly, the fact that he grew up surrounded by the smells, sounds and feel of food, and that his French mother was a very fine cook, clearly gave him a head start in the culinary stakes.

For Roux, family life and many friendships are largely conducted round the dining table, which has led to a real dislike of TV dinners, convenience and snack foods – 'all of which mean that people don't talk and savour the food together'. As a family the Rouxs try whenever possible to switch off the TV.

French families often give small children, no matter how young, little sips of bubbly on special occasions, and he thinks he first tried champagne at a wedding when he was around 5 or 6. Although raised in England, Roux's upbringing was more French than English, especially with respect to the importance attached to wine as part of the meal. Hence Muscadet, in his mind, was always a natural accompaniment to seafood whilst Burgundy went with a boeuf Bourguignonne and Beaujolais with charcuterie. Though he has gone into food and wine matching in more depth since, his love of wine remains unchanged.

Another constant for him is his unceasing (and time-consuming) quest for top ingredients, whether they come from France or Britain. In fact, he cites one of the biggest improvements in Britain over recent years as being that the country now provides a lot of wonderful produce.

At home he cooks – guess what? – simple food. Lots of plain roasts, cheese and organic food. As he puts it, 'The last thing I want to do is spend hours in the kitchen when I'm at home'.

He likes most wines, even some English ones, so long as they're well made, and his only real dislikes are (perhaps oddly for someone with his roots) the traditional French drinks Pastis and Ricard – 'They ruin my mouth for several hours afterwards' – and the French cheeses Brillat Savarin and Gratte Paille, which he dismisses as 'too creamy'.

Tartare of sea bass with dill

SERVES 4

500g sea bass fillets
2 shallots
1 small bunch fresh dill
salt
3 tablespoons full fat Greek yoghurt
juice of 1 lime
green Tabasco to taste

The sea bass, needless to say, must be very fresh:
it is also better to use larger fish as the texture will be better.
I prefer to use green Tabasco for this recipe as it is fragrant and not quite so strong,
also this must not be used until the very last minute otherwise
it will burn the fish and change its texture.

Rinse the fish, remove all bones and skin, then dice and put in a bowl set on ice.
Peel and finely chop the shallots and dill and add to the fish.
Season and fold in the yoghurt, lime juice, Tabasco and salt.

Serve with hot toasted brown bread, little gem lettuce leaves seasoned with a nut oil,
and lemon juice. If you're feeling extravagant, add a generous spoonful of caviar!

It is often forgotten that champagne is a wine, and an extremely versatile one at that.
I very often drink it throughout the meal. There are certain styles that can accompany white meats
with creamy sauces, fish courses, and desserts. More surprisingly it makes a happy marriage
with a lot of France's majestic cheeses. But for me, a champagne such as the Dom Pérignon '98
with a lightly spiced tartare of sea bass is heavenly.

For me the most important part of my cuisine is the taste, I find beauty in the raw ingredients
and get more pleasure from simplicity than "clever" artful creations.

Angela Hartnett

The Connaught

Angela Hartnett is usually described as a protégée of Gordon Ramsay, and she has certainly cooked in some of the world's most renowned kitchens – Aubergine and Pétrus to name just two. She is also often referred to as the new Elizabeth David, which, given that the latter was more of a writer than a cook, is presumably because of their shared fascination with Mediterranean flavours and foods.

Though Hartnett was born in Canterbury she has Italian blood on her grandmother's side and the family used to go to Italy quite a lot when she was young, introducing her to the Italian culinary tradition in the process. 'In my family we never need much of an excuse to sit and have a meal together,' she says. Very Italian …

Her first experience of champagne was with a rosé at a New Year's Eve celebration as a child, and although her sommelier has more responsibility for pairing wines with food, when they change the menu they always work together to make suggestions for diners seeking guidance. Their recommendations tend to be general rather than specific, suggesting an overall style of wine that would suit the dish – say, a sauvignon blanc or a full-bodied Barolo – more than individual wines, though they're perfectly happy to give exact recommendations if requested.

Whilst Hartnett obviously cares deeply about the food she serves, she also knows that there's more to the eating out experience than what's on the plate. Atmosphere and service are crucial. 'The restaurant should feel like a home from home,' she says. To that end, she always tells her managers to imagine the restaurant is their house, into which they have invited the customer who should be treated as a treasured guest.

At home, Hartnett cooks food that is quick and easy, cheese sandwiches or bowls of pasta. Anything, frankly, so long as it doesn't use coconut or coriander or is washed down by a big, buttery chardonnay.

Raspberry and champagne jelly

SERVES 4-6

7 leaves gelatine
750ml (1 bottle) champagne
2 punnets raspberries
50g sugar
2 teaspoons fresh lemon juice

Prepare the raspberries, keeping 5 per portion to place through the jelly.
Place the rest in a pan with the sugar and lemon juice,
bring to the boil and leave to simmer until reduced
to a thick purée. Let the purée cool.

Soak the gelatine in ice cold water until soft.
Warm half the champagne until just hot,
then dissolve the gelatine.
Add and mix in the rest of the champagne
and pass the liquid through a sieve.

Divide the purée into the bottom of chilled flute glasses. Allow the jelly to half set,
then pour into the flute glasses over the whole raspberries:
this allows the raspberries to set through the jelly.
Chill until set properly, and garnish with fresh mint and vanilla ice cream.

"We don't collect wine - we drink it."

PHILIP GREEN BY LUCIA VAN DER POST

You might expect Philip Green, as the owner of Britain's largest privately-owned retailing consortium and master of much of what he surveys, to be a fussy eater dedicated to the high life. But you'd be wrong. His relationship to food is entirely uncomplicated.

He's a creature of habit, he says, and likes the simple food he's used to. His only problem is that he finds it hard to say no and, by his own admission, it's made him somewhat larger than he'd like. He loves the Jewish tradition of the Friday night family meal together, and as he works in London but lives in Monaco, Friday nights herald his arrival back home, with the family sitting down with something like roast chicken, roast potatoes and a really good crumble. Comfort food par excellence ...

Whilst he could clearly afford to eat out every night of the week in some of the world's most expensive restaurants he hardly ever does so except for work engagements, preferring where possible to eat at home.

His first taste of champagne, when he was in his teens, wasn't love at first sight, but he's bravely persisted and learned to acquire a taste for it. These days he drinks it on special occasions and has learned to appreciate the finer brands. 'Once you've tasted really fine quality wines or champagnes then it's very hard to drink anything of lower quality,' he muses.

Along with his developed love of champagne he is very partial to fine red wine, particularly top Bordeaux, and he has something of a collection though, as he puts it, 'we don't collect wine – we drink it'.

As for his last supper, he'd share it with his wife and family in his garden in Monaco overlooking the sea. It would be a huge medley of all his favourite dishes, starting with freshly grilled sardines, followed by spicy marinated lamb with crispy roast potatoes washed down with one of the special reds from his cellar, and rounded off with cheesecake and a rhubarb crumble.

" Sleep, sleep, beauty bright, Dreaming o'er the joys of night"

WILLIAM BLAKE

Sir Roger Moore
by Sophie von Hellermann

Bright

ness

D om Pérignon Vintage 1998 sparkles like an effervescent gem, chuckles like a spring. Light fashions its bubbles into gilded pearls: an unfastened necklace cushioned on a shining dress of yellow tulle – a moment's splendour captured in all its candid gaiety – a rite's luminous precision. An illumination.

Brightness

Martin Blunos

THE LYGON ARMS

Martin Blunos' record with coveted Michelin stars is impressive. He won two at his own restaurants in Bath and Bristol, and has recently earned a star for The Lygon Arms where he is currently Head Chef.

His cooking is said to have Latvian touches, and there may be something in this. Though he grew up in Bath his family originally came from Latvia, and it was his mother's cooking that really inspired him to become a chef. As a boy, there was never what he called fancy food, no turned vegetables or anything fiddly, just hearty, peasant food. But nothing was wasted and much of it was cooked all in one pot. Being brought up on dishes like pig's tail soup with a jar of gherkins and rye bread may well have influenced Blunos at a subliminal level. But he feels that his real passion for cooking only started once he'd gone through catering college and was working in a small restaurant in London, where he drove his superiors to distraction with constant questions about how and why everything was done. Cooking was no longer a job for him, it was a passion.

He thinks food is one of life's great sensual experiences – almost sexual in its intensity. And whether it's a 'quickie' snack eaten on the run or an eight course gastronomic seduction, for him each has its place. Perhaps that's why his approach to food has changed a great deal over the years. To begin with he wanted 'to get as much onto the plate as possible and to do things that were difficult or unusual'. Now, he finds his cooking is becoming simpler.

'It's almost as if I've been there, seen it, done it and got the T-shirt. Now I can refine it,' he says. He is intrigued by trying to simplify dishes and says that if he could get away with putting just three ingredients on the plate, then he would. This, he feels, is the direction in which cooking is going now, and he's all for it. Sourcing the finest produce is much more important than what you do to it. Being able to make something really simple that still 'sings' is, in Blunos' view, the sign of culinary perfection.

One ingredient that's never likely to hit the top spot for him, however, is tripe, which he 'just can't get on with', despite having tried it in every style there is. Nor is he a big fan of massive, extracted red wines. 'Maybe it's just a lifestyle thing,' he muses. 'If you eat more lightly then you tend to drink more lightly.'

Scrambled eggs with caviar and blinis

SERVES 4

Blinis
450g plain flour
2 teaspoons salt
2 teaspoons caster sugar
1 teaspoon caraway seeds, ground
grated zest of quarter of a lemon
6 eggs, separated
300ml soured cream
600ml milk
7g fresh yeast
1 teaspoon groundnut oil
1 teaspoon clarified butter

Scrambled egg
4 duck eggs
1.5 tablespoons cold water
1 teaspoon unsalted butter, softened
1 pinch freshly ground white pepper
4 teaspoons caviar
100ml vodka
1 teaspoon caster sugar

Make the pancake batter first. Sieve the flour into a bowl with the salt and sugar,
then add the ground caraway and lemon zest. Mix the egg yolks with the sour cream, milk and yeast,
pour the liquid onto the flour mixture, and mix well to make a smooth batter
(if it's a little dry, add more milk – it should be the consistency of thick cream).
Cover the bowl with cling film and leave to prove for one hour, until it is bubbling and has doubled in bulk.
Finally whisk the egg whites into soft peaks and fold them gently but thoroughly into the batter,
then leave to rest for another 20 minutes.

Heat a non-stick frying pan and add the groundnut oil and clarified butter.
Brush the oil from the heated pan over the inside of four metal rings of the kind used for poaching eggs.
Pour a ladleful of the blinis batter into each ring and cook gently for 2-3 minutes,
until the tops of the blinis have bubbles over the surface. They should be about 1cm thick.
Remove the rings, flip the blinis over with a palette knife and cook for another two minutes.
Make the blinis in batches and transfer to a cooling rack, repeating until all the mixture is used up.

For the egg filling, using a serrated fruit knife carefully score and mark a line across the top of the eggs
about 1cm from the narrow end. Carefully crack open the egg so it breaks along the scored line.
Pour out the eggs into a bowl. Wash out and dry the shells: these will be used for serving the cooked eggs.

Beat the eggs in a bowl with the water, softened butter and milled pepper.
Pour the eggs into a pan and cook gently over a medium heat until softly scrambled, ie a little undercooked.
Spoon the scrambled eggs into the clean dry shells, leaving enough room for the extra topping.
With the eggs in metal egg cups or stands, heap a teaspoon of the caviar on top of each filled shell.

For the vodka flourish, warm the vodka and stir in the sugar until it has dissolved.
Pour a little of the sweetened vodka onto the saucer below the eggs.
Set this alight and serve immediately with the blinis and an extra shot of chilled vodka.

David Nicholls

MANDARIN ORIENTAL HYDE PARK

Since arriving at MJU in the Millennium Hotel, Danish chef Tom Thomsen has established the elegant restaurant's no-choice tasting menu as one of the capital's most interesting culinary experiences. Noted for his light touch, Thomsen describes his cooking as 'not fusion, but French with an Asian twist'.

Whatever you call it, his deft pairings of delicately-spiced dishes ('Oysters marinated in ginger and mirin' to name but one) with wines chosen by the sommelier has made it a great addition to the London gastronomic scene.

Thomsen can trace his culinary inspiration back to when he was 16, which was when he first ate in a fine French restaurant. It was then that it occurred to him that cooking was more interesting and complex than he'd previously appreciated, and that he'd like to make exploring flavours and textures his career.

He first tasted champagne on his 18th birthday and though he can't recall the vintage, he can recall the name on the bottle: Dom Pérignon. While this might have been a fortunate exposure to quality wine at an early age, his interest in matching food and wine was generated a little later during a year's sommelier training near Strasbourg in Alsace. The region is justly famous for its food and wine, and Thomsen travelled and explored its gastronomic possibilities extensively, working in kitchens and visiting vineyards.

He's determined not to become a 'big, fat chef', so when he cooks at home he tends to favour salads and grilled fish, though he also likes to explore Asian and sometimes Indian food. He tends to go through cycles of being intensely interested in one style of cuisine for a few months and then moving on to the next, which explains why his food tastes are wide-ranging and eclectic.

Caramelised lobster and Wagyu beef

SERVES 4

850g Wagyu beef
1 x 600g Scottish lobster
200ml chicken stock
2 rock oysters
rock salt
a few leaves baby spinach
25g Oscietra caviar

Caviar sauce
20ml vodka
juice of half a lemon
10g Oscietra caviar

Coulis
10g wild rocket
20g asparagus

Parmesan foam
100ml milk
100ml chicken stock
50g grated Parmesan

Caramelise the lobster in a pan, sear the Wagyu beef hard in a separate pan,
combine the two ingredients, add a knob of butter, then deglaze with the chicken stock.

To prepare the caviar sauce, reduce the vodka to a syrup
then add the lemon juice and caviar and blend to a smooth sauce.
Strain, leave to cool and set aside.

For the coulis, peel the asparagus and liquidise with the rocket in the blender.
Strain and set aside.

For the Parmesan foam, bring the ingredients to the boil in a pan,
then blend, strain, and set aside.

Separately warm through the coulis and the caviar sauce,
and whip the Parmesan sauce to a foam with a hand blender.
Garnish the plate with the coulis and caviar,
then arrange the oyster, Wagyu beef and lobster on the plate;
finishing with rock salt and sauces.

Why this dish marries well with Dom Pérignon 1998:
The creaminess of the '98 vintage highlights the lobster flavours in the dish,
whilst the pinot characteristics come through to the high natural richness of the Wagyu Beef.
The flavours of both the wine and the dish combine for the lingering aftertaste.

Jeff Baker

POOL COURT RESTAURANT

Jeff Baker of Pool Court, Leeds, is widely recognised as being one of the best chefs working in the North of England. But don't take our word for it. Ask Archbishop Desmond Tutu, Colin Powell, Bill Clinton, Mikhail Gorbachev or Neil Armstrong, all of whom he has cooked for.

Coming from a family with eleven cousins and six brothers and sisters, his mother and grandma were very careful in making sure that all their children were properly fed. Simple English fare and carefully-made puddings were the answer, and the importance of eating together was paramount. Even today, Baker finds himself going over to his parents for Sunday lunch most weekends, and he remains a subscriber to the 'food needn't be complicated' school of thought.

His first taste of champagne came when he was too young to be drinking it, but that didn't make it any less appropriate or memorable. It was in 1974 when Middlesbrough won the second division, and was a particular treat for his father since it was the first time that his chosen football team had ever won anything at all.

When Baker moved into the culinary premiership with his first Michelin star nine years ago, the restaurant's owner generously offered to pay for him to go anywhere in the world for dinner. He opted for the Boulis Bakery, at the time one of the most highly rated restaurants in New York. He sampled a nine-course tasting menu with different wines for each course, all lovingly explained by the Aberdonian owner. It was then that he really began to realise what an important role wine and champagne could play in the dining out experience.

Working six days a week and not returning home until midnight means that he doesn't cook much for himself, but he does like to get the children together and do a big pork roast on a Sunday. His only dislikes are the fast-food chains and, oddly for such a traditionalist, mashed potato.

Chilled rhubarb 'soup' with poached strawberries and a champagne granité

SERVES 4

Soup
400g rhubarb
16 best strawberries
2 glasses organic orange juice
stock syrup: 125g sugar dissolved in 250ml water
25ml shot of grenadine
1 vanilla pod, split
lemon balm

Granité
500ml champagne
juice and zest of one lemon
125g sugar

To prepare the granité put 125ml of the champagne in a pan with the sugar, lemon zest and lemon juice.
Heat to just below boiling point, then remove from the heat and leave to stand for 30 minutes to infuse.
Add the remaining champagne, then place in a large bowl and leave to cool. Once cooled whisk vigorously.
Leave the whisk in the bowl and place in the freezer. Whisk vigorously again every 30 minutes until frozen and granular.

For the soup, peel and cut the rhubarb into 16 batons, each 8cm long, keeping the trimmings.
Wash and trim the strawberries. Warm the stock syrup, orange and vanilla in a pan,
then add the rhubarb batons and trimmings and poach until tender. Remove and transfer the batons to a flat tray,
then poach the strawberries in the liquor and remove with a slotted spoon once tender.
Add the strawberries to the tray with the rhubarb and put the tray in the fridge to chill.

Liquidise the poaching liquor (including the rhubarb trimmings) then pass through a fine strainer or sieve.
Leave to cool before chilling in the coldest part of the fridge overnight.

To serve, pre-chill the serving bowls. Place the rhubarb batons and strawberries in the bowls,
then pour the chilled 'soup' over them. Select the smallest leaves from the lemon balm as garnish: finally,
spoon some of the granité into the centre of the soup and serve immediately.

"I was sitting on my balcony eating baked beans: they were amazed."

SIR ROGER MOORE BY LUCIA VAN DER POST

Roger Moore doesn't need much of an introduction. His urbane manner and suave good looks have been indelibly connected with the de luxe lifestyle since his days as James Bond. So it comes as something of a shock to find that, away from the spotlight, the real Roger Moore loves the simplest of foods.

'People are often surprised,' he says. 'Once Michael Caine and Leslie Bricusse rang me and, when they asked what I was doing, I said I was sitting on my balcony eating baked beans: they were amazed.' Presumably champagne and caviar was more what they were expecting.

Moore has happy childhood memories of his mother's wonderful cooking, most particularly of her sensational steak and kidney pie, the creation of which was limited only by the fact that, as a teenager during the Second World War, the weekly meat ration was meagre. 'We would have a tiny little joint on Sunday which would appear cold and thinly sliced on Monday and then in bubble and squeak on Tuesday,' he recalls. He still remembers his first visit to America after the war and being stunned by the size of the hamburgers.

He was equally stunned during his National Service in Germany when he had to look after three silos full of confiscated German army supplies. Amongst them were hundreds of bottles of champagne, all with swastikas on them. 'Well, I quickly condemned them and we were soon drinking them,' he says, though since this was his first taste of champagne, he found the taste hard going to begin with. 'Since then I've been lucky enough to go to Reims and Epernay, and to drink champagne that has never ever been moved but has spent all its life in one place,' he says. 'That is very special. You realise then what fine champagne is all about.'

When he did The Persuaders series with Tony Curtis, the two actors managed to persuade the 'powers that be' to let them drink proper champagne instead of the watered down tea that usually passes for it in the theatre. 'If you watch you'll see that I put on about two stone through the series,' he says drily.

For him food is important in the sense that it is often over food that he sees his friends and family, but his tastes these days are fairly simple. Indeed, during the frantic whirl of the social season with all its balls and dinners, he often finds himself yearning to put his feet up in front of the TV with 're-runs of Upstairs Downstairs and some lovely vegetable soup or a boiled egg'.

As we've seen he loves baked beans, and he's also rather fond of Sainsbury's veal and ham pie with a boiled egg in the middle. 'I'm not difficult to feed you see,' he says with spectacular understatement!

In fact, the only sort of food he really doesn't like is what his daughter calls 'poncy food' that has been fiddled with so much as to be quite unrecognisable on the plate, though he's not keen on strawberries or peaches – and he absolutely hates coriander. Chicken curry is a big favourite of his, and he'd probably ask for either that or steak and kidney pie like his mother used to make as his last ever meal, along with 'all the things that I really shouldn't eat for it wouldn't matter any more.'

With the chicken curry he would have an ice-cold lager, and to finish he'd have either gorgonzola or Stilton with a glass of port. As a grand finale, he'd love an old-fashioned Walls choc ice, the sort they don't make any more with dark chocolate on the outside and vanilla ice-cream inside.

James Bond would be horrified, but Roger Moore, it seems, is quite content.

"Space
is seamless"

ALBERT EINSTEIN

Theo Fennell
by Sophie von Hellermann

Seamless

ness Sea

The legendary smoothness of Dom Pérignon flourishes in the clasp of Dom Pérignon Vintage 1998's fervent embrace. A flood of exquisite sensations caresses the taste buds: a moment of weightlessness, followed by velvety notes vibrating to the muted echo of a zest of lime. An abrupt, acerbic coolness persists, like the pedal note of a perfectly performed Bach fugue.

mlessness

Simon Radley

The Chester Grosvenor and Spa is in the heart of Cheshire's old-money belt, and many of its customers come looking for the traditional luxury dining experience: caviar, foie gras, truffles and lobster. It's the job of Executive Chef Simon Radley to give it to them.

As a boy, he was attracted to the profession not by the idea of conjuring up magic with the world's finest ingredients, but by the opportunity to wear a big white hat. While he's embarrassed by his admission, he maintains that it was absolutely true. He was enormously impressed at seeing people who were obviously important taking a pride in what they were doing. Chefs, he felt, had a chance to express themselves every day of the week, whereas in most jobs men were told what to do and had to get on and do it. He loves the work, and can scarcely believe his luck.

For Radley, good food and wine are one of the glues that hold social life, families and friendships, together. Many business deals and most friendships, he points out, are forged over the dinner table, while meal times are one of the main ways the family is able to get together and talk properly to each other.

When he first tried champagne he thought that it was destined to be just a rich man's pleasure and to his delight he's found this isn't true. In his line of work he now comes across it on a daily basis and he's been fortunate enough to cook for the Champagne Academy three times.

He takes pairing food and wine seriously. He works closely with the sommelier and they do food and wine pairings at least once a month. He likes to think that they're getting quite good at it, but part of the charm of the task, he realises, is that it is a very subjective matter and there's always bound to be someone who disagrees with their findings.

Veal sweetbread with poached lobster tail, chickpea, almond and spice

SERVES 4

2 x 500g lobsters
4 x 275g veal sweetbreads, blanched & skinned

250g pasta flour
5 egg yolks
1 egg
pinch of saffron strands, steeped in hot water

Mild curry sauce
10g turmeric
2g chilli powder
5g cardamon pods
5g fennel seed
5g cumin seed
5g coriander
200g blanched almonds
mirepoix vegetables: 1 each carrot,
onion & celery stalk, diced

500ml fish stock
500ml whipping cream
500g chickpeas
250ml chicken stock
12 pak choi leaves (or spinach)
curry oil
olive oil

Blanch the lobsters in boiling water for 4 minutes, then chill and shell.
Separate the claws, split the tails in half and remove the entrails.

Mix the pasta flour, saffron water, egg yolk, a pinch of salt and a splash of olive oil.
Knead together, then rest the dough for an hour before rolling out to the finest setting on a pasta machine.
Cut into strips 25cm long by 5cm wide. Blanch and refresh.

Roast the curry spices in a dry pan then crush the mix.
Sweat the mirepoix in hot oil, then add a pinch of the curry spice.
Sweat again, add the fish stock, and reduce the liquid by half.
Add the cream and reduce again by half, then finely strain the curry cream.

Toast the almonds in foaming butter until they are golden brown, then remove and sprinkle with salt.
Cook the chickpeas in the chicken stock until they are soft, then purée and strain, keeping back a fifth for garnish.

Fry the sweetbreads in foaming butter until they are golden and cooked through.

Reheat the lobster in a butter and water emulsion: warm the pasta in salted water
with a splash of olive oil and wrap one sheet around each sweetbread.
Sit the pasta on seasoned chickpea purée in the centre of the plate.
Blanch the pak choi or spinach leaves and arrange on the pasta, topped with half a lobster tail and a claw.
Reheat the cooked chickpeas and almonds and scatter them around the plate.

Dress with curry oil and the curry cream, foamed with a hand blender.
Decorate the plate with toasted cumin and coriander seed.

John T Williams

John Williams is lucky enough to preside over what is generally recognised as one of the most attractive dining rooms in the world, and one which everyone should experience at least once in their lifetime: The Ritz London.

He has happy early childhood memories of scraping Jersey Royals for his mother for Sunday lunch and, later, being inspired by the Galloping Gourmet. 'I'd watch Graham Kerr go to all these beautiful restaurants, where he would always be dining with a wonderful woman, and I remember thinking "I could do that"' he says.

He remembers tasting champagne for the very first time at a birthday celebration when he was about 14. The bottle in question was Pol Roger Brut, and he remembers splitting the cork and putting a 50 pence piece in it. He has the cork to this day.

Williams takes great pleasure in pairing up food and wine, but it wasn't until he became a chef, when he had more exposure to clients and had to discuss menus in earnest, that he really began to become deeply involved in the process. 'Sometimes when you're a chef you can really be put on the spot, and I realised that I had to understand wine better,' he says frankly. 'That's the reason I went on some courses to try and learn more about it.'

He believes very much in using seasonal ingredients and only the freshest, finest quality that he can find. After that his approach is to use classic combinations but to give them a modern tweak. As with most chefs, when he's off duty his diet involves lots of vegetables and salads. 'The older I get, the more simply I like to eat,' he says. This simplicity does not include anchovies, which he dislikes even in a Caesar salad, or Beaujolais Nouveau.

Braised pork belly
with Dublin Bay prawns and onion coulis

SERVES 10

1.5kg pork belly
2.5kg onions
100g carrots
80g celery
80g celeriac
1 litre chicken stock
half a bay leaf
1 sprig thyme
1 star anise
2 cloves garlic

100ml cream
10 extra large Dublin Bay prawns
2 litres court bouillon
300g Oscietra caviar
100g butter
1 bunch chervil

Slowly bake 3 large unpeeled whole onions in a tray covered with foil for 2 hours.
Allow to cool slightly; then remove the skins and reserve.

Peel, chop, and sweat the remaining vegetables in a little olive oil.
Once slightly softened place the belly pork on top, pour on the stock and bring to the boil.
Add the herbs and spices, cover with foil, and braise gently for two and a half to three hours.
Once totally cooked through take out the meat, remove the skin, cut into regular rectangular portion sizes, and reserve.

Bring the braising liquor to the boil and reduce to a syrup, then pass through a fine sieve.
Bring back to the boil and add the cream and simmer gently to a sauce consistency.

Place the baked onions in a blender with the cream sauce and blend: this will produce a thick coulis.
Place in an espuma, add gas to the siphon and reserve the coulis.

Cook the langoustines for 2 minutes in the court bouillon, ensuring it is highly salted, then peel immediately.

To serve, siphon some of the espuma onion coulis onto the centre of the plate.
Place a piece of pork belly on top, arrange the langoustines, and finish with chervil and caviar.

John Campbell
THE VINEYARD AT STOCKCROSS

John Campbell is on record as saying, soon after his arrival at The Vineyard at Stockcross, 'sometimes you have a great kitchen, sometimes you have a great restaurant; this is the first time I've had both.' For somebody who didn't train under a great Michelin-starred chef and who developed his own style of cooking, the restaurant has been a stunning success, retaining its Michelin star and winning accolades by the hatful.

He learned a lot from his grandmother, with whom he lived for about three years in one of the poorer districts of Liverpool. She did wonders with cheaper cuts of meat, dried beans and the other bits and pieces that were all she could afford. 'She had this way of producing something great out of almost nothing,' says Campbell admiringly. To this day he thinks some of the ways she cooked are worth remembering. For instance, for Sunday lunch they wouldn't have a roast joint but boiled ham, gammon or hock. His grandmother would buy it on the Friday, soak it overnight, cook it on the Saturday and cook cabbage and butter beans in the juices. His grandfather, meanwhile, was in charge of the potatoes. He would boil them until they were just disintegrating, then turn them in hot beef dripping, put them in the cold oven and leave them there overnight where they would absorb all the flavour from the dripping. On Sunday morning he'd fire up the oven and out would later come magnificent roast potatoes. To the small John Campbell it seemed like a miracle.

His first taste of champagne came at a big family party one New Year's Eve when he was about 9. Before then he'd only ever been offered Babycham, but that night his father gave him proper champagne for the first time and he remembers it to this day.

His appreciation of food and wine matching began many years later when the general manager at a hotel where he was working brought in a wine specialist. Together they would ask Campbell to taste wines at lunch and decide what worked best with the different dishes, which really forced him to concentrate.

These days he believes there are two ways of looking at wine's role with food: it can either support a dish, or it can work with it. For example, with something quite light he might suggest a bold, supporting wine, whereas with a rich risotto he would tend to prefer a sauvignon blanc, where the wine's acidity tempers the dish's fatty richness.

No doubt about it, wine is important to him. At The Vineyard, he has instituted wine suggestions for every single dish, with comprehensive notes from the sommeliers. And following a tasting at Dom Pérignon he's looking at more ways to match champagne with food. His approach to cooking is, he admits, quite complicated, what he calls a search for 'alternative vehicles to deliver the flavour.' Tomatoes, for instance, could be prepared fresh, as a jelly, as a crisp, fried, cooked, half-cooked or confit, and all would taste very different. His aim is to find the 'vehicle' that enables him to get the optimum flavour out of each ingredient.

At home he likes to eat outdoors wherever possible. If it's summer they'll usually start to eat at about 4pm and not finish until somewhere around 7. In winter he'll cook dishes with deep flavour, not unlike those his grandmother used to cook in Liverpool all those years ago.

Salmon 'mi-cuit', spiced lentils, foie gras ballotine

SERVES 4
with plenty of spiced lentils and chutney
for another occasion

Spiced lentils
350g puy lentils
30g pickled ginger, finely chopped
2 medium red onions,
   peeled & finely chopped
4 cloves garlic, crushed
half a teaspoon ground cumin
100ml balsamic vinegar
100ml soy sauce
4 tablespoons tomato ketchup
6 tablespoons sweet chilli sauce
50ml olive oil
30g fresh coriander chopped
salt & pepper

Fig and apple chutney
1 cooking apple,
   peeled & cut into 2cm dice
20g onion, diced
50g dried figs, chopped
25ml white wine vinegar
a third of a tablespoon English mustard
pinch of Cayenne pepper
half a clove garlic
50g sultanas
sugar

Foie gras ballotine
500g foie gras
5g pink salt
   mixed with
2.5g table salt
2.5g sugar
10ml Madeira
10ml port

Vanilla oil
2 Tahitian vanilla pods
100ml corn oil

Salmon 'mi-cuit'
1kg salmon fillet
a splash of whisky
100g each salt & sugar

Salmon 'mi-cuit'
Remove the skin, blood line, bones and cartilage from the salmon and cut into 60-70g portions.
Season with the mixed salt and sugar and a splash of whisky.
Leave this on the salmon for 3 hours, then wash off, dry and store the salmon.
Cook the salmon in an oil bath set at 45°C for 30 minutes, when it will be ready.
Lightly season with salt flakes before serving.

Spiced lentils
Cook the lentils in salted sparkling water, then drain and cool.
Sweat the onions in the vinegar with the cumin and garlic for 10 minutes,
then add the rest of the ingredients and correct the seasoning.

Fig and apple chutney
Combine all the ingredients in a heavy saucepan. Bring to the boil, then lower the heat and simmer
for 2 hours until thick: add a splash of water if the mixture dries out before the 2 hours are up.
Leave to cool, then briefly liquidise the mixture until it has the consistency of jam. Store in the fridge.

Foie gras ballotine
Place the foie gras in a plastic bag, expelling all the air before sealing, and immerse in cold water
until it is soft to the touch, a soft butter consistency. Remove and split the foie gras into its two lobes.
De-vein, trying not to split the skin, sprinkle the salt mix and alcohol in the middle,
and wrap tightly into a ballotine ensuring there are no air pockets.
Leave in the freezer to set overnight.
Pan fry the foie gras until golden all over. Re-wrap in cling film, once again ensuring there are no air pockets.
Place in a preheated oven at 56°C for 8 minutes, then refrigerate before cutting and serving.

Vanilla oil
Scrape the seeds out of the pods. Warm the oil to no more than 40°C: this will allow the vanilla to infuse into the corn oil.
Infuse for 2 hours, then remove the pods and store the oil.

To finish the dish, heat the lentils and slice the foie gras. Place the chutney on top of the foie gras.
Dress the plate according to your own style: the key to this dish is that the flavours combine well with each other
as long as the chutney is on top of the foie gras.

Tom Aikens

TOM AIKENS

Tom Aikens first registered on London's foodie radar when he was working at Pied à Terre, and since the opening of the restaurant that bears his name in Elystan Street his reputation has continued to grow.

In a sense, he was introduced to food through wine. His father was in the wine business and would combine business and holidays in France, with the result that his son was exposed to good cuisine at a very early age. He remembers going to a very chic one star Michelin restaurant at the age of 16 when nouvelle cuisine was at its height. While his parents loved eating frog's legs, he, perhaps unsurprisingly, tended to plump for steak frites.

Like many culinary professionals he regrets what convenience food has done to eating habits, though he believes that a backlash is under way and that more people are now trying harder.

Given that his father was in the drinks trade, his first taste of champagne was relatively late – 11 or 12 – but having visited numerous vineyards as a child he did grow up with an inherent appreciation of the importance of pairing good food with good wine. The latter, incidentally, doesn't include Blue Nun, which he strongly dislikes.

His approach to cooking is to combine unexpected tastes and flavours in search of a new and exciting culinary experience, though this doesn't extend to when he cooks for himself at home when simplicity is the order of the day. 'You don't want to be doing much cooking if you've spent all day in a restaurant,' he says, with hard-to-fault logic, though if he's entertaining he'll happily head off to Borough Market and spend all day on the meal.

Salad of peas and Parma ham

SERVES 4

600g shelled fresh peas
2 leaves gelatine
caster sugar
200ml double cream, semi-whipped
small bunch of mint
2 long shallots, finely diced
3 punnets pea shoots
4 slices Parma ham

Dressing
1 egg yolk
zest and juice of 2 lemons
225ml olive oil

Soak the gelatine leaves in cold water. Cook two thirds of the peas in boiling salted water for about four minutes
with a large pinch of sugar and salt to taste, then drain and plunge into iced water. Leave for a few minutes, then drain.

Cook the remaining peas in the same way, retaining their cooking water, then place this last third in a blender with 150ml
of the cooking water. Add the soaked gelatine and make a purée. Pass this purée through a fine sieve,
then transfer to a bowl and store in the fridge. Stir from time to time until it has nearly set, then add the cream,
which should be the consistency of thick custard. Season, and add a tablespoon of chopped mint:
you may also need to add a pinch of sugar or a squeeze of lemon juice. Then chill.

To make the dressing place the yolk in the blender with the lemon juice and zest, then blend for a minute.
Slowly add 200ml of olive oil, and a little water if it gets too thick, season, then add a pinch of mint.

Cook the shallots in the remaining oil until soft but not coloured, then place in a bowl to cool.
Add the cooked peas and another large pinch of chopped mint, with a little dressing to bind them together.

Arrange the shallot and pea mixture on the plate with a little dressing, then the pea mousse, pea shoots and Parma ham.

Simon Haigh

MALLORY COURT COUNTRY HOUSE HOTEL AND RESTAURANT

Simon Haigh is Head Chef at Mallory Court in Royal Leamington Spa, where his cooking is much admired for the lightness of his touch and what the Egon Ronay Guide called his 'mastery of textures'.

Although no single thing drove him into cooking, he feels it was probably a combination of having a mother who always cooked well – and had no time for convenience food – and his being fairly non-academic and always wanting to do something with his hands. He fell into cooking almost by accident, found it relatively easy, and has enjoyed it ever since.

He reckons that he probably first tasted champagne with his wife because she used to have her own hotel. Her grandfather only ever drank Moët & Chandon, but at all times, and it was rude not to join him whenever he suggested cracking open a bottle. A few headaches were the price paid for his heroic politeness.

He generally leaves the question of choosing the right wines to go with the menu to his sommelier, though in fact Haigh isn't too keen on highly proscriptive rules. In his book people should drink what they like; he has no time for stuffiness.

For Haigh, seasonality is paramount, and he tries to use ingredients when they're at their peak. He wouldn't serve strawberries in the winter and he doesn't use frozen food. Not only are seasonal ingredients cheaper, he argues, but they taste better as well; more people should adopt this approach.

At home he doesn't cook at all and – most unusually for a chef – he and his wife live on take-aways if they're not eating out at one of the many gastro-style pubs in their area.

Garigette strawberry crème brûlée

SERVES 6

100g garigette strawberries
6 eggs
115ml caster sugar
550ml double cream
1 vanilla pod, split

Cream the eggs and sugar until light. Bring the cream to the boil with the vanilla and pour over the egg mixture.
Strain into a mould and cook in a bain-marie for 40 minutes at 160°C till set, then leave to cool.

When cool, cut out into portions with a cutter and glaze with sugar using a blowtorch.
Use the same cutter to arrange strawberries on the plate, place the brûlée on top,
and serve immediately with ice cream or sorbet and the coulis of your choice.

"Champagne is about all that it stands for, what it evokes and what it does to the imagination."

THEO FENNELL BY LUCIA VAN DER POST

Theo Fennell, the jeweller to the stars, is well known for his wonderful parties. He is, by all accounts, one of the best hosts in London. And yet he himself no longer drinks at all. 'I drank lots until about five years ago and then I started feeling not so well when I woke up and I thought – hang on here, it's a hangover. I'd better give it up.'

The irony is that, now that he doesn't drink, he serves better wines and champagnes at his table and his parties than ever he did before. 'I lavish fine wines upon my friends. I think it matters hugely. The thing is, people think if you don't drink that you're going to be mean and serve them rubbish. Ever since I started buying wine I've gone to Johnny Goedhuis – he knows a whole more about it than I do and it's saved me having to learn. I leave it all to him.'

In his drinking days he loved champagne. He was introduced to it very young because his father, who was a soldier, loved it before him. 'He used to have one champagne in the morning – then a different one for the afternoon', he recalls. Fennell serves a great deal of champagne at his own parties (rosé in the summer) because, while the drink itself is magnificent, for him it's about more than just the liquid in the glass. 'Champagne is about all that it stands for, what it evokes and what it does to the imagination.'

His tastes in food are very eclectic. Because his father was a soldier he discovered exotic cuisine at a very early age. He lived in Malaya, Thailand, France and Pakistan, and loves dishes like nasi goreng (which he describes as an Asian form of paella) and kedgeree. He remembers to this day the first curry that he was given in Malaya, and lamb rogan josh is one of his all-time favourite dishes. The only food he really can't understand is raw fish – 'I simply can't see the point of it' – but cooked Japanese food he loves.

If he were putting together the ingredients for his last meal he'd make sure it was with his wife, either at home in front of the telly or in a Corfu villa overlooking the Albanian coast that they take every year.

He would start with little bits of breadcrumbed grilled sole and he'd like them served with a white egg sauce. He would follow this with a very thin fillet of medium-rare steak, accompanied by a lettuce salad and a tart dressing and some perfectly done French fries. For pudding there would be a pistachio crème brûlée followed by coffee and as many chocolates as he could manage.

"A charming woman ... doesn't follow the crowd. She is herself."

LORETTA YOUNG

Lord Lloyd Webber
by Sophie von Hellermann

Char

robing the aromas, the flavours, the textures of Dom Pérignon Vintage 1998 for the secrets of their chromatic affinities and their sumptuous harmonies, a mysterious alchemy is unveiled. Invocations, enchantments, sensuous ecstasies combine in a bewitching commemoration of their strange, unforgettable correspondences.

Charm

Christine Manfield

For Christine Manfield, cooking was third time lucky. She started off her working life as a teacher, then became a hairdresser, before finally realising that the kitchen was where she truly belonged.

Extensive travelling helped in her culinary education, of course, but her interest in global food began before that when, as a student, she lived with other students from around the world and began to realise that there was a whole world of different culinary traditions out there, all of which had something individual and interesting to offer. As a naturally adventurous person, she tried as many as she could.

Her first taste of champagne was a glass of Krug at a birthday party in Adelaide, so it's perhaps no surprise that she confesses to being a bit of a champagne snob who refuses to drink sparkling wine from anywhere else in the world.

She didn't realise quite how important – or, indeed, exciting – matching complementary wine with food could be until she started cooking professionally. The fact that her first job as a chef was at a newly opened restaurant associated with Petaluma, the iconic Australian winery, wouldn't have done her education any harm …

The hallmark of her cooking is a sense of adventure. She has always loved to travel, and that desire to be challenged and stimulated (one of the reasons she came to London) is mirrored in her food.

At home, unlike most chefs who prefer to keep things simple, she likes to use the same sorts of flavours, with just as much complexity, as she does in her restaurant, albeit with fewer dishes. She'll eat almost anything except kidneys – 'I'm not fond of renal failure' – and the only thing she asks when others cook for her (which she loves) is that they season the food properly. She likes most foods and most styles of wine: she just doesn't like anything mediocre. Or, as she puts it in her forthright Australian way, 'I don't like crap'.

Crispy pork and black pepper squid with cashew salad

SERVES 4

400g steamed pork belly,
  cut into 3cm cubes
1 teaspoon Szechuan spice salt
200g squid tubes,
  cut into thick strips & finely scored
3 tablespoons black pepper salt crust
vegetable oil for deep-frying

Chilli caramel

zest & juice of half a sum saa (Asian lime)
250g palm sugar
100ml tamarind liquid
100ml fish sauce
1 cup fried shallot slices
1 birds eye chilli, minced

Salad

4 tablespoons cucumber julienne strips
2 red shallots, sliced in two lengthways
2 teaspoons fresh young ginger,
  cut into fine julienne strips
1 long red chilli, sliced into fine rounds
4 tablespoons coriander leaves
2 tablespoons Vietnamese mint leaves,
  shredded
4 tablespoons mint leaves,
  finely shredded
4 tablespoons cashew nuts,
  boiled & deep-fried till golden
4 tablespoons fried shallot slices
4 tablespoons fried garlic slices
4 iceberg lettuce leaves, finely shredded
4 betel leaves, shredded

Red chilli dressing

3 large coriander roots
2 small garlic cloves
3 red bird's eye (small) chillies
50g caster sugar
minced zest of half a sum saa
100ml lime juice, strained
25ml clementine (or mandarin) juice,
  strained
25ml fish sauce

To make the red chilli dressing, pound the coriander, garlic and chillies with a pestle and mortar until finely smashed.
Add and pound the sugar, then add the lime zest, juices and fish sauce. Taste and adjust the seasoning if necessary.

For the chilli caramel, heat all the ingredients together in a pan and simmer for 10 minutes until slightly reduced.

To cook the pork and squid, heat the vegetable oil to 180°C and deep fry the pork cubes for 1 minute until crisp.
Remove from the heat and toss with Szechuan spice salt.
Toss the squid strips in the black pepper crust and deep fry for 30-40 seconds until crisp, then remove from heat.

To make the salad, combine all the ingredients in a bowl with the crisp pork and black pepper squid,
add sufficient chilli caramel and red chilli dressing, in equal quantities, to coat the mix and toss with the hands to combine.
Arrange the salad on serving plates and finish with a few extra fried garlic slices.

Andrew Turner

1880 @ THE BENTLEY KEMPINSKI
LONDON

There are some meetings that change your life. For Andrew Turner it was bumping into the renowned Albert Roux. He'd already been a chef for seven years when he ran into the great man, and ended up working for him at Hanbury Manor. In his first week he was introduced to four or five of Roux's dishes that completely changed the way he thought about what food was and what it could be. It introduced him, he says, to 'cooking with the heart and not the brain'.

Now chef at 1880 in The Bentley Hotel in South Kensington, he has become famous for his 'grazing' menu, which offers eight or nine small dishes all culled from the main à la carte menu. It has proved hugely popular and has, as one critic put it, 'injected new life into the often tired world of dining in a hotel restaurant'. He describes his style of cooking as a 'deconstruction of classic food followed by a reconstruction of those same ingredients, but in a contemporary style'. Not that he is wedded to the artistic or esoteric approach. He makes sure that his children and family eat only the best quality ingredients, if possible sourced locally, and cooked simply. Food, he maintains, doesn't have to be grand to be good.

He remembers drinking champagne for the first time: he was only 9, and it was at his sister's wedding. Enthusiastic in his attempts to get to grips with the mystery of the world's finest sparkling wine, this was the first time he was ever told off by his parents for being drunk.

His understanding of food and wine matching really took off when he was working with a sommelier called John Gilchrist at 1837. They had 350 wines available by the glass (for which they quite rightly won an award) and were keen on promoting seven- to ten-course menus, with each course paired with a particular wine. He learned a lot working on developing these ambitious menus, and was fascinated by the way wine could change the character of certain dishes. He likes to think of the menu as a journey that can have many different final destinations, depending on the foods and wines chosen.

Turner's approach to food may sound complicated, but he claims that it is actually quite simple at heart. He likes using the best seasonal ingredients and tries to highlight their flavour while doing as little as possible to them. He believes in Marco Pierre White's dictum: 'Keep it simple and do it well'.

Although he has a passion for Chinese and Thai cuisine, he's not so keen on fusion food and at home tends to cook a lot of roasts, which are his wife's favourite. When it comes to wine, he is particularly fond of wines from Burgundy but also Australia and New Zealand. 'In fact,' he admits, 'there aren't too many wines I don't like.'

His pet hate is chefs who try to apply Heston Blumenthal's science-based approach to food without really understanding the principles. 'Heston can get away with it – he knows what he's doing,' he says. 'But other chefs have bastardised and debased his ideas. If you have your own way of cooking you should stick with it. Be a master of one thing and don't try and be an all-rounder. That's exactly the same approach that our friend Dom Pérignon had, was it not?'

Celtic sea scallops
with cauliflower, capers, and raisins

SERVES 4

12 extra large King diver scallops
1 medium cauliflower
100ml virgin olive oil
icing sugar
250ml full fat milk
125ml double cream
20 x 5cm lengths baby leek
250g unsalted butter
chervil for garnish
salt & pepper

200ml fish cream sauce
80g salted capers
80g golden raisins

Prise the scallops from their shells with an ordinary table knife.
Separate the scallop from the roe and remove and retain the beard (it looks a little like tripe), which will be used for the sauce.
Place the scallops unwashed on a tray as diver scallops contain no sand: only scallops
that have been dredged (which we don't use!) need washing.

Take off the cauliflower florets. Cut each floret across the middle into very thin slices all of the same width:
they should look like mini white trees. Dust them liberally with icing sugar and pan fry in a little olive oil until golden.

Cook the rest of the cauliflower in the milk with salt to taste until tender.
Remove from the cooking liquor and dry in the oven until no steam is visible,
then liquidise in a food processor using the double cream as a thinning agent.
Adjust the seasoning to taste, and then leave to hang for a few hours in a muslin bag.

Cook the baby leeks in boiling salted water until tender, then refresh as normal.

To serve, dry the scallops on tissue paper and cook quickly in a splash of olive oil on the stove to your required degree.
Spoon the cauliflower purée onto the plate and place the scallops on top.
Garnish with the fried cauliflower florets and buttered baby leeks, decorate with chervil and serve.
I accompany this dish with a caper and raisin sauce, my European version of sweet and sour.

Neil Perry

THE ROCKPOOL, SYDNEY

Neil Perry started cooking at the age of 19 at Sails restaurant in Sydney, but made his name at the Blue Water Grill at Bondi – 'all surf, sand, and sauvignon blanc' as he puts it. The Blue Water Grill's success was based on simple food and an eclectic menu with lots of Asian influences. He found even more fame with his Rockpool restaurant, now partnered by Wockpool in Darlinghurst. In his spare time he oversees the menus and training for Qantas airlines.

These days Australia is renowned for its gutsy and innovative approach to food, particularly in bridging European and Asian cuisine, but when Perry was growing up his father's passionate interest in food and in the provenance of ingredients was distinctly out of the ordinary. His father was a butcher and very keen fisherman who also grew vegetables in his garden, so Perry was introduced at a very young age to the importance of really fresh high quality ingredients. Indeed, this is where he believes his interest in food came from, not least because his father used to gather his children round the table to think about and evaluate the food they ate.

He can't remember his first taste of champagne, but can certainly remember his first encounter with Dom Pérignon. He was just 19 at the time, and it cost a ridiculous A$14. 'We had a great exchange rate at the time, about eight francs to the dollar and no import taxes, so Dom Pérignon was fantastic value,' he says with a certain amount of understatement. These days a bottle of Dom Pérignon would set you back about A$180.

Through his parents, who encouraged him to share their passion for good food and wine, he was introduced pretty early on to the notion that the right wine could enhance the pleasure of a meal. As young as 11 or 12 years old he would have a glass of watered-down riesling, and by the time he was 16 he would be taking a glass of wine with most meals; the two simply always went together.

For Perry, flavour and texture are the most important considerations when preparing food and, like his father, he believes that provenance is all. He likes to know the fishermen personally, to be sure they're treating the caught fish correctly, so that by the time it reaches his kitchen it is in the best possible condition. At home he cooks the sort of food he rarely makes in the restaurant, from simple Mediterranean-style dishes through slow-roasted joints to stir fries with noodles or a pot of red curry.

Fresh Iranian Oscietra caviar with spawn custard

SERVES 6

180g fresh Oscietra caviar

Spinach oil
1 bunch English spinach,
 stems removed
sea salt & freshly ground white pepper
180ml extra virgin olive oil

Custard
250ml eggs (about 4 x 55g), whisked
250ml prawn stock
1 teaspoon fish sauce
1 teaspoon palm sugar

Prawn stock
100ml olive oil
1kg green prawn shells
half a small onion, finely diced
1 small carrot, finely diced
2 cloves garlic, minced
half a small leek, washed & finely diced
125ml brandy
125ml port
250ml dry white wine
250ml chicken stock
4 vine-ripened tomatoes, blanched,
 peeled, de-seeded & finely chopped
half a bunch thyme, leaves only
half a bunch tarragon, leaves only

Cauliflower purée
50ml olive oil
50g unsalted butter
half a small onion
1 clove garlic, minced
sea salt & freshly ground pepper
half a cauliflower, cut into small pieces
200ml chicken stock
juice of 1 lemon
120ml extra virgin olive oil

For the spinach oil, steam the spinach leaves for 5 minutes over rapidly boiling water.
Squeeze out excess water and blend, adding salt, pepper and olive oil, to a very smooth purée.
Leave the purée to infuse for an hour then pour into a few layers of muslin, squeeze out all the oil, and discard the solids.
Finally strain the oil through a fine sieve and store at room temperature until ready to use.

To prepare the prawn stock heat the oil in a heavy-based pot on the stove until very hot.
Add the shells and stir for 5 minutes until coloured, then add the onion, carrot, garlic and leek and cook for a further 5 minutes.
Add the brandy and reduce until it almost disappears: add the port and reduce, then the white wine, continuing to reduce until almost all the liquid has gone. Pour in the chicken stock and add the tomatoes and herbs.
Lower the heat and cook for 20 minutes: don't allow the stock to boil again.
Pass the sauce through a food mill, then through a fine strainer.

For the cauliflower purée put the olive oil and butter in a heavy-based saucepan and heat until the butter foams.
Add the onion, garlic, and a little salt and cook until soft but not coloured.
Stir in the cauliflower, then add the chicken stock and cook for about 15 minutes over a slow heat:
don't let the sides or bottom burn or the cauliflower will discolour.
Keep stirring, especially towards the end as the liquid cooks away.
When all the liquid is gone, blend to a purée, slowly adding lemon juice and extra virgin olive oil
to lighten the texture. Season with pepper and cool to room temperature.

Preheat the oven to 130°C. Whisk the eggs for the prawn custard;
pour in the prawn stock and whisk until completely incorporated.
Season with the fish sauce and palm sugar and skim the foam off the surface.
Spray 6 small dariole moulds with Pure and Simple (or lightly oil),
then pour the custard mix into the moulds and place in a bain-marie with hot water.
Cover the top loosely with foil and cook in the oven for 30-40 minutes:
the custard will appear set on the outside but will still be runny in the middle.
Remove before it sets too firmly, allow to cool, and refrigerate until required.

Spread a spoonful of cauliflower purée into the middle of six large white plates.
Run a knife around the edge of the dariole moulds and turn out the custard onto the centre of each plate.
Drizzle spinach oil around the outside and place 30g of caviar on each. Serve immediately.

Pascal Aussignac

CLUB GASCON

For some people Pascal Aussignac's Club Gascon is London's finest restaurant, not just because of the quality of the food but because it is genuinely regional. While many eateries offer 'classic with a twist' or national cuisine, Aussignac's homes in on the tastes and textures of Gascony. His is a cooking that knows its roots.

No surprise, then, that his interest was first kindled by helping his mother in the kitchen, and he can still remember creating some 'way-out' pizzas with a savoury shortbread base that was very light and fragile. Now, he thinks good food is 'everything'.

He remembers his first taste of champagne very clearly. It was Christmas 1978, he had gone skiing, broken his leg on the first day, and spent the whole of the holiday in hospital. But he remembers his uncle visiting with a bottle of champagne, which they drank on the bed. It certainly helped cheer up the 11 year old invalid.

He started seriously to pair food and wine when he opened Club Gascon. In September 1998 they introduced a menu du marché to sit alongside the à la carte menu. Changing every month, it consists of a five-course meal made from seasonal ingredients, with each dish paired with a different glass of wine, and has been enormously popular, accounting for half of all the restaurant's orders.

Such an idea may have been common in France, but when it started Aussignac's Menu du Marché was unusual in the UK. Since then many other restaurants have adopted the idea, for one simple reason: it works. Those without specialist wine knowledge like it because the choice is taken out of their hands, while oenophiles enjoy the chance to try a wide range of wines.

For Aussignac, the most important part of his work is to track down the best food producers then pass on their passion for quality to the customer.

At home he doesn't cook very much at all, beyond the odd barbecue, because his kitchen is so small. So when not entertaining friends he leaves most of it to his girlfriend. There's very little he dislikes apart from rice pudding (which he hates) and cheap, mass-produced wines.

Warm aromatic foie gras, hay sauce

SERVES 4

1 fresh duck foie gras (around 600g)
500g dry fragrant wood, eg vine
500g hay (available at pet shops)
100g grapeseed oil

Prepare the foie gras and separate 50g. Store both parts in the fridge

Spread the wood over a grill tray and dry it in the oven: use a blowtorch to help the wood start to burn.
When the wood has turned to embers, lay 550g of the foie gras on the grill over the tray.
Cover with a lid and allow it to smoke for 5 minutes, then put the smoked foie gras back in the fridge.

For the sauce, just cover the hay with water in a large pan.
Boil until you have a very strong hay-flavoured reduction, about 20ml.
Take out the hay and transfer the reduction and the 50g of foie gras to a blender:
slowly add grapeseed oil until the sauce comes together. Season to taste with salt and pepper.

A few minutes before eating, slice the foie gras using a knife dipped in hot water.
Season the slices and put them in a very hot non-stick pan: do not add any oil or butter.
Cook the slices for 2 minutes on each side. Serve warm with the hay sauce.
Both flavours will perfectly complement the Dom Pérignon 1998.

Giorgio Locatelli

LOCANDA LOCATELLI

Giorgio Locatelli's family ran a Michelin-starred restaurant in northern Italy, so he has been surrounded by good food for as long as he can remember. 'In the morning,' he says now, 'people talked about what they were going to have for lunch, and in the afternoon they'd talk about what they were going to have for dinner.'

With food so much a part of his life, it was always odds-on that he would go into the restaurant business, and the difficulty of obtaining a table at his current eatery bears out the esteem in which he is now held. Like most chefs, he believes that eating well is one of the keys to a good life. Although, as he points out, 'there's not much point in eating so well that you have diabetes by the time you're sixty!'

He has good reason to remember his first encounter with champagne. His grandfather was born on December 31st, which ensured a big party every New Year's Eve in the family restaurant. When he was 7 he was deemed old enough to be given a bottle of champagne to open. He was so excited at such an honour that he threw the bottle up to the ceiling, caught it, and then opened it. The moment he took the cage off it exploded and hit him in the eye, giving him a black eye that lasted three weeks.

Working in rather grand kitchens and being a chef's chef, Locatelli tended to work apart from sommeliers and took no real interest in the pairing of wine and food until he started to create his own dishes. Until then, preparing somebody else's food, he'd tended to keep his head down and concentrate on producing it to the standard they asked for. Worrying about the wines that might match the dishes didn't come into it.

He has taken more of an interest in wine since he opened his own restaurants, but is wary of being over-didactic when it comes to recommendations. He's in the service industry, giving people whatever will give them pleasure; he doesn't believe in food fascism. Nor does he believe in over-elaboration. 'I'm really trying to pass true flavours on to my customers, rather than trying to mush it all together and put sixty five things in a dish to show how clever I am.'

At home his wife does most of the cooking, but if it's his turn he'll probably do a nice barbecue, making sure everything is of the best quality. They don't shop in supermarkets, buying all their meat from specialists, and Locatelli will drive a hundred miles out of London just to get some beech wood for a cook-out. 'If you pay less, it usually means you get less,' he says simply. His dislikes include pretentious food, restaurants that look down on their customers, and spicy or very complex white wines.

Strawberry and mango lasagna

SERVES 4

3 mangoes
500g strawberries
100ml water
200g sugar

2 stackable shallow plastic containers

Peel and slice the mango, making sure the slices are as thin as possible.
Keep the trimmings: not the stone or peel, but all the pieces you were not able to slice thinly.
Clean and thinly slice the strawberries.

Line one of the shallow plastic containers with cling film.
Spread a layer of mango slices over the cling film, followed by a layer of strawberry slices.
Repeat until all the fruit has been used.
Cover the whole surface of the lasagna with cling film and place the other plastic container
on top of the fruit as if you were trying to stack both containers.
Turn both upside down, place the equivalent of a 2kg weight on top,
and store in the fridge for at least 12 hours. Liquid will drip from the lasagna,
so make sure there is a large plate under the containers.

Boil the sugar and water in a pan until the sugar has dissolved to make a stock syrup.
Meanwhile blend the mango trimmings to a purée; add syrup to the mango while the blender
is still running until you have a shiny sauce. Add more syrup to taste.

Take the lasagna out of the fridge. Turn it upside down, remove the first container
and turn it upside down again onto a chopping board, making sure you peel the cling film layers off.
Cut off the edges and divide into four portions.
Arrange on the plate and spoon the sauce over the top: eat immediately.

"an impressive command of the nuances and subtleties of the high culinary arts."

To the armies of fans more used to thinking of Andrew Lloyd Webber as a weaver of magical musicals, it was perhaps something of a surprise when, in the pages of a national newspaper, he turned out to be an extraordinarily perceptive and authoritative commentator on food and wine. His scholarly weekly reviews were masterpieces of their type and showed an impressive command of the nuances and subtleties of the high culinary arts.

Those with a passionate interest in food seem mostly to have been inspired in one of two ways: either they are introduced to it by keen foodie parents, or they are consistently served dreadful meals and turn to cooking in desperation to get something edible. For Andrew Lloyd Webber it was most definitely the latter. 'My mother and grandmother were probably the worst cooks I knew,' he says.

Salvation came in the form of an understandably much-loved aunt, Viola Johnstone, his mother's sister, who was a minor celebrity chef in her day and with whom the young Lloyd Webber spent many a happy holiday in her Tuscan home. 'I really got to know about food and wine through her,' he says now. She was a wonderful cook who produced several books and introduced her hungry nephew to the delights of authentic Italian cooking and the country's wine. By the time Lloyd-Webber was a teenager he was already quite an accomplished cook, and still remembers happy meals with his aunt at the old Portofino restaurant in London's Camden passage.

He, in his turn, has made sure that his children share with him the delights of the table and made a point of taking all his children to restaurants as soon as they were old enough to behave properly.

These days the family has a house in Mallorca, which he reckons has become the foodie capital of Europe, and where he loves to cook. 'I sold the home I'd had for many years at Saint Jean Cap Ferrat because it had changed out of all recognition,' he says sadly. 'When we first went there there were about eight great restaurants that we could simply walk to from the house. By the time we left there was just one.' In Mallorca he takes great delight in trawling the markets for great ingredients, and in taking the family out to enjoy the first-rate restaurants found all over the island.

Perhaps surprisingly, he isn't a great lover of champagne, preferring white Burgundy. And while he's prepared to eat both the head and tail of a suckling pig, he has a strong aversion to marzipan.

When it comes to how he would spend his last night on earth he says it would be with his wife Madeleine at La Grenouille in New York. 'It's remained solid and true to its French roots, and reminds one of how great French cooking used to be,' he says. He would start with quenelles de brochet accompanied by a Beaune Clos des Mouches, then a poulet grandmère with a 1947 Cheval Blanc. Not much of a pudding fan, he'd probably finish with some cheese and a 1969 Romanée-Conti.

"God made
a very obvious
choice when
he made me
voluptuous;

why would I go against what he decided for me? My limbs work, so I'm not going to complain about the way my body is shaped."

DREW BARRYMORE

Meredith Etherington-Smith
by Sophie von Hellermann

Voluptuous

Volu

The substance – dense and profound – of Dom Pérignon Vintage 1998 slides full-bodied over the lips, then cascades over the palate in a series of rapturous epiphanies. In the dilatory insouciance of wine-tasting, that Bacchic ceremony of suspended time, the entire gamut of the god's rich treasure trove pours out in a magic instant of pleasure and delight.

ptuousness

Andreas Antona

SIMPSON'S RESTAURANT

Besides Simpson's Restaurant, Michelin-starred chef Andreas Antona has recently opened a contemporary bistro in Kenilworth called Simply Simpson's. In both venues, he and his team concentrate on producing exquisite dishes that are firmly rooted in the French classical tradition.

With his parents running an eatery in Bayswater, Antona more or less grew up in a restaurant and nearly all his childhood memories are to do with food. He thinks some of life's most agreeable pleasures revolve round the family table and restaurants are, in his view, an extension of that, offering a trouble-free way of getting together with friends or family.

His first taste of champagne came when he was about 12 at a party given by one of his parents' friends, and he remains interested in wine to this day. He and his sommelier, Jerome, are committed in their search for wines that enhance the food so they can pass this information on to their customers.

For him, cooking is simple: a case of using the very best ingredients, then preparing them with love and care. He doesn't go in for anything elaborate at home, cooking for himself what he calls 'plain stuff'. This 'plainness' doesn't, however, include tofu, which he hates, and wouldn't dream of serving in any restaurant of his.

Tronçonettes of lobster, coconut basmati rice, apple, sultanas, and curry sauce

SERVES 4 as starter, 2 as main course

2 x 800g lobsters

Curry sauce
40g butter
60g chopped onion
1 pineapple, finely diced
1 apple, finely diced
1 banana, chopped
grated coconut
200ml coconut milk
300ml chicken stock
1 shallot, finely diced

Coconut rice
200g basmati rice
50g onion, finely chopped
200ml milk
200ml coconut milk
25g butter

Apples and sultanas
2 Braeburn apples
50g sultanas
25g butter
sugar

To prepare the curry sauce, melt the butter in a saucepan, add the onion, and cook until soft.
Add the pineapple and apple and cook for 5 minutes.
Add the coconut, coconut milk, banana and chicken stock, bring to the boil, and simmer for 30 minutes.
Transfer to a blender and blend until smooth. Pass through a fine sieve and season with salt and pepper.

For the rice, cook the onion gently in the butter until soft. Add the rice and cook for a further 3 minutes.
Add the milk and coconut milk, bring to the boil and add a pinch of salt.
Cover with a tight fitting lid and cook very gently for 10-12 minutes.
Remove the lid to stop the cooking and reserve in a warm place.

Cover the sultanas with boiled water in a bowl to soak, then leave to cool.
Peel and cut the apples into small cubes, then heat in a small pan with the butter and a pinch of sugar.
Cook until soft, add the sultanas, and reheat.

Kill the lobsters by inserting a heavy knife into the top of the head between the eyes.
Remove the heads and claws.
Bring a large pan of salted water to the boil and cook the claws for two and a half minutes.
Remove with a slotted spoon and refresh with iced water.
Repeat for the tail, cooking for 30 seconds only.
Crack open the claws and carefully remove the meat.
Divide the tail into four, cutting along its natural lines.
Place the tail and claws on a grill tray, season with salt and pepper and drizzle with olive oil.
Place under a hot grill for approximately 4 minutes until just cooked.

To finish, spoon the rice onto the plate, place claw meat on top of the rice and the tail down one side of the plate.
Sprinkle sultanas and apples down the other side, spooning curry sauce around the lobster.

David Dandridge

THE BERKELEY

David Dandridge fell in love with food on a boy scout camping trip. The sausages may have been burned and the potatoes only baked on a grill, but something clicked, and he's been attracted to the culinary arts (albeit at a rather more refined level) ever since.

He sees food not just as a great way of socialising, but also as a way of getting a tantalising glimpse into the culture of other countries and peoples. 'As chefs, we don't just cook where we live, we cook all over the world,' he says philosophically. 'We live the world, in terms of food.'

His first taste of champagne came as a young commis chef at the Savoy Hotel in the early 1970s doing a big cocktail party. Silvino Trompetto ('a legend' Dandridge calls him) was the executive chef at the time and since there was a lot of champagne swilling around, insisted that they try it. 'So I did – and I've never looked back,' he says.

His approach to food is very open-minded, whether supplying well-done steak or accepting that not everyone likes raw fish. Not everyone, he realises, is as adventurous as he is. With twenty years travelling and working all over the world under his belt, he's tried all manner of weird and wonderful dishes, from mopane worms in South Africa ('OK with tomatoes'), iguana eggs in Venezuela (drawn straight from the recently-killed iguana) and bat stew in Indonesia. The only thing he has really disliked is a strange dish from the Philippines which consists of a fully formed duck inside an egg. He had to crunch down the whole thing, black beak and all, and although it was meant to be an aphrodisiac he really didn't enjoy the experience.

When he's at home the eight years he spent living in South East Asia often come out in his cooking. And his wife, he says, is a fantastic cook, at least as good as he is. He concludes, 'If everything is quality-driven, then it gives everybody the chance, the guest and the chef, really to produce the best and enjoy the best. Poor quality is something I just don't want to be associated with'.

Creamed Dolcelatte with honey truffle

100g Dolcelatte
20g Mascarpone
1 teaspoon of clear honey infused with shaved Alba truffle

Salad
2 small handfuls young watercress tips
a few sprigs baby wild rocket leaves

Dressing
a few drops 12 year old balsamic vinegar
one tablespoon new season freshly pressed extra virgin olive oil

Cream both the cheeses together, then form into two quenelle shapes.

Scatter the salad leaves, which have been dressed by lightly combining the oil and vinegar,
over large Artisan glass plates. Arrange a cheese quenelle on each plate.
Finally, drizzle thin threads of truffle honey.

The taste highlights of the dish are the slight saltiness of the cheese offset by the sweet honey,
and followed immediately by the perfume of the truffles. The crunchy salad leaves need no salt
because of the cheese, and no pepper because of the rocket and watercress.

Allan Pickett

GREAT EASTERN HOTEL

Allan Pickett has gained an enviable reputation for his cooking at Aurora, in the Great Eastern Hotel, and is especially well known for his approach to game, which he serves in all manner of irresistible combinations … grey partridge with a pithivier of wild mushrooms, Savoy cabbage and cep jus to name but one of his specialities.

He became interested in food and cooking when very young because every Sunday his mother and grandmother would involve him in preparing the big weekend meal. While he notes that for much of the population the whole 'sitting down and eating together' ritual has been lost, he's determined to make sure that when he has a family they will enjoy meals together, particularly at weekends.

Like most chefs he started his working life very young, and it was probably when he was at catering college, aged 16, that he first drank champagne. The drink has always had a vital role to play in toasting life's anniversaries and achievements, and he always has a few bottles stashed away at home for when friends come round or there's something to celebrate.

As a chef, spending his working life with food, he finds that the wine you drink with food matters, and if he goes to a top-notch restaurant he's happy to take guidance from the sommelier. He's not against trying unusual combinations (or trying champagne with food either) working on the reasonable basis that 'if you don't taste, you'll never know'. When trying out dishes that would go well with the Dom Pérignon 1998, for instance, he found that a sea bass dish they devised complemented the wine wonderfully, whereas a frog's leg truffle dish didn't work at all.

His cooking is based on the classical French techniques of braising, stewing, and poaching, but with a modern approach when it comes to combining ingredients. As trends in food change, Pickett reckons, the hallmark of a good chef 'is that he is able to re-interpret old classics in his own way without jumping on every bandwagon that comes his way'.

At home, Pickett goes for simple food as long as it's of high quality and full of flavour: quiches, roast chicken or stew are all favourites, even when he's entertaining. His tastes are fairly eclectic and there isn't a lot that he doesn't like, apart from deep, heavy red wines, and cauliflower.

Pavé of wild sea bass,
truffled celeriac purée, pinot noir jus

SERVES 2

2 pavés of line-caught wild sea bass (about 175g each)
1 small celeriac
400ml milk
2 cloves garlic
1 small Périgord truffle (enough for two people)

Pinot noir jus
250ml pinot noir wine
750ml good brown chicken stock
a sprig thyme

Begin by peeling and cutting the celeriac into a small dice, then cook with the milk and garlic until it is very tender.
When cooked, drain and reserve the milk, as it may be needed to loosen the purée slightly if it is a little too thick.
Blend the celeriac in a liquidizer until smooth, adding some of the cooking liquid if needed.
Once finished add a little of the sliced truffle to the purée and adjust the seasoning.

For the jus, reduce the wine to a syrup in a pan, then add the chicken stock and reduce by two thirds.
Add the thyme and take off the heat to cool as the thyme infuses, then strain through a chinois. Reheat before serving.

Roast the sea bass and place on a warmed plate alongside the celeriac purée with the jus spooned around.
Finish by shaving the truffle over the plate and serve immediately.

Kenny Atkinson

THE GREENWAY

Kenny Atkinson, Head Chef at The Greenway hotel in Cheltenham and famed for his duck confit, first became attracted to a chef's life not because of the food but because of the buzzy atmosphere. He was doing a part-time job in a hotel, wandered into the kitchen, took one look at the frenzied goings-on and thought, 'Yeah, I can do this'.

He remembers tasting champagne for the first time at the first important restaurant that he ever worked in, the Mandarin Oriental in Hyde Park. He took his then girlfriend, now wife, out for her birthday – the first serious meal that either of them had ever had – and he still remembers that the chef, Howard Jones, really looked after them and went all out to give them a fantastic experience. He gave them a big tasting menu and they had champagne and a different wine for each course. It opened their eyes to what food was all about and reinforced Atkinson's fascination with the world of food, chefs and kitchens.

He works closely with his sommelier to try and match his dishes to good wines. Every season they change the menu and when he finds a new dish they always get the restaurant staff to taste it and see what they think. He also consults with the restaurant manager or the sommelier and asks them to try and recommend a wine or champagne that would enhance it.

He is broadly optimistic about the way food is treated in Britain, thinking that people are becoming generally more interested and critical about what they eat and that eating out is growing in popularity. He's naturally a big believer in using ingredients when they're at their best, and his restaurant is well known for its use of local produce, building menus on seasonal principal ingredients and working around them, trying to 'lift' without overwhelming.

At home he loves simple, hearty food, nothing too fancy – things like shepherd's pie, spaghetti bolognese, or pasta – 'and certainly won't cook at home the sort of food I cook in the restaurant'.

Honey glazed belly of free range pork, creamed celeriac purée, baby onions, buttered asparagus, caramelised apples and pan-fried langoustines

SERVES 4

Belly of pork
1 small belly of free range pork
2 carrots, peeled
2 leeks, washed
1 head celery, washed
1 bulb garlic, split in half
400ml white wine
1.5l chicken stock
half a teaspoon fennel seeds
half a teaspoon coriander seeds
10 white peppercorns
2 star anise
1 small tin whole peeled plum tomatoes
2 sprigs rosemary
2 tablespoons runny honey

Garnish
16 langoustines
16 English asparagus spears
16 small baby onions, peeled
4 Granny Smith apples
16 baby morels
16 crosnes
4 black pudding discs 5cm wide,
  1cm thick
lemon oil
Maldon salt

Celeriac purée
500g celeriac, peeled & diced
3 shallots, peeled & finely sliced
3 cloves garlic, peeled
1 slice bacon
300ml milk
300ml double cream

Red wine sauce
1 bottle red wine
4 banana shallots, finely diced
1 clove garlic, crushed
2 teaspoons redcurrant jelly
1.5l veal stock
1.2l braising liquor from belly

To braise the pork belly, first remove the bones and place them in a deep dish. Season the belly with salt and pepper, then carefully roll it into a large sausage shape and tightly tie with butcher's string to help retain the shape. When the belly is tightly tied, place in the braising dish and cover with the roughly chopped vegetables and all the remaining belly ingredients except the honey. If the meat is not covered by liquid add either more stock or a little more water. Cover the dish with either a lid or tin foil and slowly braise for 4-5 hours at 160°C. When the time is up remove the pork from the oven and allow it to cool in the liquid. When the belly has cooled remove from the stock and place in the fridge to chill overnight. Pass the stock through a fine chinois and reserve for the red wine sauce.

To make the celeriac purée, cover the garlic, shallots, bacon and celeriac with the milk and cream and simmer until soft. Remove and pass the celeriac through a sieve, then transfer to a blender and blend, slowly adding a little of the liquid, until a smooth thick purée is achieved. Pass the purée through a fine sieve to make it even more smooth and velvety, then season with salt and ground white pepper.

For the red wine sauce simply add a knob of butter to a pan and slowly sweat the shallots and garlic until soft and translucent. Add the red wine and reduce right down to a syrup. Add both the veal and reserved pork stock to the syrup with the redcurrant jelly. Reduce the sauce until thick and glossy, then pass through a muslin cloth to remove any impurities. Reserve the sauce until needed.

Remove the pork from the fridge and slice into 7cm lengths, then with a sharp knife carefully trim away the outer fat to leave a perfect ballotine of pork. Season the meat with salt and pepper and pan fry in a little vegetable oil until nicely coloured on all sides. Add a good knob of butter and two tablespoons of runny honey and place the pork in the oven at 180°C for 10 minutes, basting frequently with the honey to help keep the meat moist and form the glaze.

To cook the langoustines simply remove the heads and 'shit line', add the tails to boiling salted water for 10 seconds, then quickly refresh in iced cold water. When chilled remove the shells, carefully wash the langoustines and place on a cloth to dry. Peel and cut the apples into quarters, remove the core, and neatly dice into 2cm cubes. Heat a little butter and a pinch of caster sugar in a pan and toss the apples until they are golden brown, sweet, and caramelised. Pan fry the baby onions in a little vegetable oil and lightly dust them in icing sugar. When they are nicely coloured finish in the oven for 8 minutes.

Peel and trim the asparagus to 5cm lengths and place in a small pan just covered with water, a knob of butter, and a pinch of salt. Quickly simmer until all the liquid has absorbed into the asparagus. Pan fry the black pudding for 30 seconds on both sides and place on a cloth to drain. In a separate pan sauté the crosnes in foaming butter until cooked, then add the morels, season, and drain on cloth. Pan fry the langoustines in a little oil in a non-stick pan until golden brown on both sides, then season, squeeze over a little lemon juice, and also place on a cloth to drain.

To serve, carefully spoon the warm purée into the centre of the plate or bowl with black pudding on top. Arrange four of each garnish - baby onion, morel, crosne, asparagus, apple dice, langoustine - neatly around the purée. Place the glazed belly of pork on top of the black pudding, neatly spoon the jus over and around the pork, and finish the dish with a little drizzle of lemon oil.

Marco Pierre White

FRANKIE'S ITALIAN BAR & GRILL

Marco Pierre White is the youngest chef in the world ever to win three Michelin stars and the only British chef ever to do so. These days he runs a mini-empire, owning the Criterion, the Mirabelle, Quo Vadis and L'Escargot. Not bad for someone who claims he only became a chef because he didn't have many other options.

As a very young boy he got a job at the Box Tree restaurant in Yorkshire, which was justifiably famous in the 1970s for being one of only four restaurants in Britain to have two stars in the Michelin Guide. Thirty years ago, that was as good as British cuisine got.

Though clearly he loves wonderful food he believes that the pleasures of the table are important for much deeper reasons than mere gastronomy. His wife is Spanish and they eat in what he calls a Mediterranean way. The food (usually seven or eight dishes) is not served already plated up, but put in the middle of the table with everybody helping themselves as and when they feel like it.

Though his children are at boarding school, they make a point of eating together when they are home for the holidays, and he and his wife always make a feature of breakfast, lunch and dinner because they feel it's important to interact with their children at the table. They certainly have no time for TV dinners, and White loves the whole ritual attached to eating all together – even chores like the washing up and clearing the table afterwards, all of which he feels is part of proper family life.

It seems scarcely credible, but White never drank at all until he was 38 when, as he puts it, 'I stopped cooking and started drinking'. No great surprise, perhaps, that he's not overly bothered about pairing food with wine. While there are certain established pairings that he accepts – Sauternes with foie gras, for example – generally, he describes the practice as 'pretentious'. And the sort of people who are interested in pairing every course with a precious separate wine are not, he thinks, the sort of people with whom he'd want to share a table.

Food, for him, is a matter of sitting down, breaking some bread together and having a good time, which is perhaps why he likes simple food. 'Mother Nature herself is the artist', he says, 'the chef is merely the technician', bringing the work of the artist to the diners. He has no major food or drink dislikes except Blue Nun.

Pannacotta with poached fresh strawberries in champagne

1 litre Jersey double cream
90g caster sugar
2 Madagascar vanilla pods split in half lengthways
25ml Jamaican dark rum
two and a half leaves gelatine

Strawberries
48 fresh English strawberries
1 bottle of champagne (Dom Pérignon '98 if you can afford it)
750g caster sugar

For the pannacotta bring the double cream, caster sugar, vanilla pods and dark rum to the boil.
Soak the gelatine leaves in water, then take the hot cream mixture off the stove, add the leaves,
pass the liquid through a sieve, and allow it to cool, stirring frequently.
Pour out the mixture into 8 moulds and leave to set in the fridge.

Bring the champagne to the boil with the caster sugar and pour the hot syrup over the strawberries. Allow to cool.

To serve, turn out the pannacotta onto a plate and spoon the strawberries around with some of their juices.

"We saw Stravinsky's 'The Rake's Progress'… and I was allowed a glass of rosé champagne."

MEREDITH ETHERINGTON-SMITH BY LUCIA VAN DER POST

Meredith Etherington-Smith, who is large, extravagant, and very funny with it, loves really good food and wine and doesn't mind who knows it. 'After all,' she says disarmingly, 'you only have to look at me'.

Her interest began young, as de facto kitchen maid to her mother who, although English, used to produce 'wonderful food of the classical French bourgeois variety, laden with garlic and herbs' for her French father. All this in the dark days before Elizabeth David when buying garlic, Parmesan cheese and avocados necessitated a special trip to Soho. 'It was the only place you could find them in those days,' she recalls.

Whilst her mother was busy making bourgeois French comfort food, her grandmother would often do the British equivalent – stews, hotpots and the like – so it's no wonder that she was thoroughly imbued with food culture before she left home. In fact, she claims to have clinched the hand of her second husband by cooking him the best grouse he'd ever had. 'It was very high and roasted with bacon and a little water, served with great game chips: he didn't stand a chance,' she says. When she moved her Magimix in he knew his fate was sealed.

She remembers with great clarity the day she first tasted champagne, when her father took her to Glyndebourne when she was just 12. 'We saw Stravinsky's The Rake's Progress and ate salmon and salads and I was allowed a glass of rosé champagne,' she says. She loves champagne to this day, though she prefers slightly sweeter versions than most Brits and often serves it as a dessert wine.

Nowadays she doesn't cook as much as she used to. 'The trouble is we're just two at home now and we're both always on a diet', but she retains a healthy hatred of junk food and is always on the lookout for 'good diet food that's a bit unexpected and interesting'. The sort of Spanish-Moroccan food served up by the Moorish-influenced restaurant Moro is a current passion, but her favourite cookery book of all time (from a less weight-sensitive era) is Mapie de Toulouse Lautrec's Classical French Cuisine. 'I've used it so much that half the pages are missing and there are notes scribbled all over the pages saying things like less butter, or more oil,' she says – surely the sign of a great tome.

She has – as you might expect – some strong views on what she likes and dislikes. She is fond of offal, but her pet hate is overcooked vegetables ('a culinary crime') and she doesn't like 'anything watery.' When it comes to wine she avoids anything German ('just not my taste') and isn't very fond of oaky chardonnay – 'I like flinty whites and big boy clarets,' she says.

Ideally her last meal on earth would take place at home with her husband Jeremy, and she'd like to have the menu that was served at his 70th birthday party. It would start with proper wild smoked salmon ('none of that pink, slimy supermarket stuff'), then there'd be a saddle of lamb, carved off the saddle, with an array of baby spring vegetables and perfectly roasted potatoes. 'Nigella Lawson's recipe is divine,' she enthuses, 'you parboil them, bash them about a bit, roll them in semolina and then roast them in goose fat.' Pudding would just be fresh English raspberries served with Cornish cream and a glass of rosé champagne. She would finish with some perfect Stilton and, instead of a glass of port, a tiny glass of Armagnac.

"I am the music
I am the
vibrant string
The sensuous
shimmer, the
soaring call ..."

FROM THE SONG OF THE BARD, ALAN KILBURN

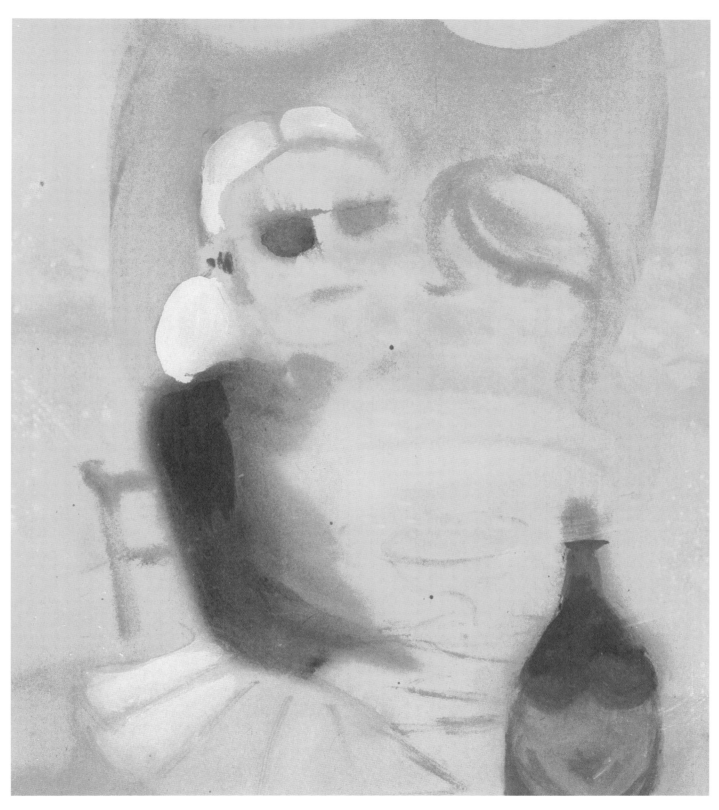

Karl Lagerfeld and Helena Christensen
by Sophie von Hellermann

Sensuous

Sen

Like a promise of endless rapture escaping from the mouth of an unstoppered vial, Dom Pérignon exudes an intense sensuality. Powerful aromas and liquid flavours are woven together into a voluptuous sense-experience, which the palate refracts spectroscopically into an infinite rainbow of mutually echoing sensations.

suousness

Steve Smith

SEAHAM HALL
HOTEL AND SERENITY SPA

Steve Smith started his career under Jean-Christophe Novelli at Provence at Gordleton Mill, where he gained a Michelin star when still just 24. He has worked in other Michelin-star properties such as Rascasse, Gidleigh Park and Longridge, Paul Heathcote's restaurant, and also won a Michelin star at Holbeck Ghyll after only eight months in the establishment.

He acquired a passion for food when he was just what he calls a 'young kid', courtesy of his grandmother's frequent and entertaining Sunday lunches. A big, social gathering, the whole family would help make the food and enjoy not just the eating but the preparation as well.

He doesn't remember the first time he tried champagne, which he assumes means that it was a good occasion. Nowadays, he tends to drink it on special occasions or as an apéritif when he goes out for dinner. Sometimes, too, he will have half a bottle (but no more) with dinner, depending on what he's eating.

Smith puts a lot of thought into pairing wine and food. The first time he sampled a complete menu paired with complementary wines was at Harvey's, Marco Pierre White's restaurant in Wandsworth. He just asked the sommelier for something that would be fantastic with each course. The expert's choices, he says, really made a difference.

He tries to keep his cooking fairly simple, with precise flavours, and while he will push the boundaries out a little bit, his experimentation tends to be with different combinations that he knows work well together. At home he cooks food that he can rustle up in half an hour – salads and simple risottos – and even if he has quite a few friends round he still tries to keep it simple. He likes to be able to plonk a great big dish in the middle of the table and let everybody get stuck in. The only thing that he doesn't particularly like to get stuck into is oysters.

Lobster ravioli, braised lamb's tongue and sweetbreads, crushed peas and marjoram

SERVES 4

Pasta
125g pasta flour
80g egg yolk

Lobster
60g lobster meat
10g salmon mousse
1 tablespoon chives
half a teaspoon lemon juice

Lamb's tongue
30g mirepoix
4 lamb's tongues
2 cloves garlic
1 sprig rosemary
500ml chicken stock

Sweetbreads
60g lamb sweetbreads,
  blanched & cleaned
1 tablespoon flour
1 tablespoon sherry vinegar
1 tablespoon nut oil
1 sprig rosemary
1 garlic clove
10g butter

Confit tomatoes
2 tomatoes peeled,
  seeded & cut into petals
1 clove garlic, sliced
1 sprig thyme
2 tablespoons olive oil

Pea purée
200g peas
5 mint leaves
50ml double cream
50ml milk

Crushed peas
100g peas
10 sprigs mint
half a teaspoon marjoram
1 tablespoon olive oil

Onion purée
200g onion, chopped
25g butter
50ml double cream

Rosemary jus
200ml Noilly Prat
200ml Madeira
2 sprigs rosemary
1 clove garlic
1 shallot, diced
15g carrot, diced
15g celery, diced
600ml lamb jus
30ml olive oil
100g lamb neck

Mix all the pasta ingredients together to form a dough, then leave to rest in the fridge for at least an hour.
Combine the lobster, salmon mousse and chives. Season to taste with salt, pepper and lemon juice.

Roll out the pasta to the thinnest setting on the pasta machine. Place four equal amounts of lobster mix 3 inches apart on the pasta. Cover with another sheet of pasta and press down around the lobster mix to seal the ravioli. Cut out with a cutter and place in the fridge.

Wash the lamb's tongues in running water for 20 minutes. Cover with chicken stock in a pan, bring to the boil, and skim. Add the mirepoix, rosemary and garlic, reduce to a simmer, and gently cook the tongues for approx 2 hours. Allow to cool. While still warm, peel the skin from the tongues. Store in some of the cooking liquid.

For the onion purée, gently melt the butter in a heavy bottomed pan and add the onions. Slowly cook until completely caramelised and golden brown. Drain all the butter from the pan. Add the cream and season with salt and pepper. Place the onions in a blender and blend until smooth. Push the liquid through a fine sieve and reserve.

For the pea purée, bring a small pan of slightly salted water to the boil, add the peas and bring back to the boil. Remove the peas immediately and place in a blender with the mint and cream. Blend till smooth, then cool over ice and store.

For the crushed peas pulse the peas, mint and marjoram in a pulse blender to a rough texture. Add the olive oil, season, and store.

Place the tomatoes for the confit on a tray. Sprinkle over the garlic, thyme and salt, drizzle with olive oil, and place in a warm area to dry out.

For the rosemary jus, sweat the carrot, celery and shallot in the olive oil until soft, then deglaze with the Noilly Prat and reduce until all the liquid evaporates. Add the Madeira, bring to the boil, add the stocks and reduce by half. Roast the lamb neck and drain off all the excess fat. Pass the stock through a chinois, place into a separate pan and add the lamb bones, rosemary and garlic. Reduce by a third.

As near as possible to serving, roll the sweetbreads in the flour and pan fry gently in warm oil. Add the garlic, rosemary, and butter. When the butter starts to foam add the sherry vinegar, remove from the heat, and baste the sweetbreads with the butter and vinegar. Keep warm.

When ready, reheat the purées. Reheat the lamb's tongue in the rosemary jus. Cook the ravioli for two minutes in a simmering pan of salted water. Spoon pea and onion purée on to opposite sides of the plate, with crushed peas in the middle. Scatter the sweetbreads and lamb's tongue around the edge of the plate, and place the ravioli on the crushed peas. Scatter the tomatoes over the top, apply the sauce, and serve.

first taste of champagne during her role in Ninotchka. The austere beauty is suddenly catalysed by a sip of bubbly into a sensuous woman in love.

Even those who don't normally drink make an exception for champagne. It's as if the usual rules don't apply. It is too beguiling, too seductive, altogether too tempting. Karl Lagerfeld knows the feeling well, "You know, I don't drink much alcohol. In fact, I only like champagne. And I'm not being diplomatic when I say that the only champagne I really know is Dom Pérignon." It was this special feeling that Karl Lagerfeld set out to capture in the photographs he shot for the campaign to launch the 1998 vintage. For Helena Christensen it was a campaign like no other. "There was a slightly erotic feeling in the air, but handled with extreme elegance. It's a bit like describing the feeling champagne gives you. Karl is extremely good at drawing out emotions and feelings. It was like shooting a scene in a film with discreetly sexy lighting and champagne as the star."

Champagne can be an initiation into a new world, bubbling with possibility and glittering with promise. People fall in love with champagne. And like a demanding lover, champagne needs to be treated right. "There are three intolerable things in life: cold coffee, lukewarm champagne and over-excited women" noted Orson Welles. Irascible old Orson was demanding with his actors, but champagne isn't such a stern taskmaster. Champagne is playful, liberating and can open up astonishing new vistas. It has an allure every bit as compelling as a Hollywood star.

Even Hollywood stars like Marilyn Monroe. It's 1959 and the Marilyn Monroe-Arthur Miller marriage is coming apart. But that night, over a glass of Dom Pérignon, another story is born. At a party in New York, Marilyn cuts through the crowd with a champagne glass in her hand, and offers it to the young Danish screenwriter, Hans Jorgen Lembourn, whom she had met a few days before.

"Here. I'll find another for myself. It's Dom Pérignon, my favourite champagne."
"How are you, Miss Magnetism?"
And so began the fairy-tale. It was to be brief, impulsive, child-like, and like all good fairy-tales, blissfully dissociated from the mundane. Forty days in pursuit of happiness, with a lovers' escapade to the mountains by car as the plotline. And, like a talisman, there is always a bottle of Dom Pérignon on board. In fact, a whole stock of bottles, in the boot, on the back seat, buried among the dresses and slacks, shirts and pullovers, scarves and shoes, make-up, bags and hats, books and curlers, stockings and peignoirs. Amidst Marilyn's chaos, a cache of Dom Pérignon, like ammunition for happiness.

We crossed Manhattan and the Hudson River. In New Jersey, we drove northward, then west, to the mountains. She started out huddled in the corner of her seat, without saying a word. Then she sat up and started rummaging through the bric-a-brac scattered on the back seat. She fished out a bottle of Dom Pérignon, opened the glove box and produced two plastic cups. She removed the capsule, then the wire and popped the cork, aiming it out the window as the foam flew in the wind. She filled the cups, handed me one, downed hers in two or three gulps, filled it again and propped the bottle between her knees. She had her cup in one hand and held onto the brim of her extravagant hat with the other.

"Now we're on vacation", she announced.

Quarante Jours et Marilyn
Hans Jorgen Lembourn, Paris, Robert Laffont, 1979

Paupiette of veal flavoured with shallot and garden herbs, Bordelaise potatoes	68
Pavé of wild sea bass, truffled celeriac purée, pinot noir jus	234
Pork: and black pepper squid with cashew salad	182
Pork: honey glazed belly with Dublin Bay prawns and onion coulis	148
Pork: honey glazed belly, creamed celeriac purée, baby onions, buttered asparagus, caramelised apples and pan-fried langoustines	240
Quail: tartlet and quail eggs with onion confit, summer truffle and smoked bacon, wild mushrooms and a light quail jus	62
Raspberry and champagne jelly	86
Rhubarb: chilled 'soup' with poached strawberries and a champagne granité	126
Salad of crispy langoustines with apple, Thai jelly and sole mousse	120
Salad of grilled duck and longans	280
Salad of peas and Parma ham	160
Salmon 'mi-cuit', spiced lentils, foie gras ballotine	154
Salmon gravlax	34
Scallop: and tuna ceviche, shaved fennel salad, Oscietra caviar with lime dressing	274
Scallop: progressive tasting ceviche	28
Scallop: tian and crab mousse	268
Scallop: Celtic with cauliflower, capers, and raisins	188
Scrambled eggs with caviar and blinis	102
Sea bass: pavé with truffled celeriac purée, pinot noir jus	234
Sea bass: tartare with dill	80
Sole: Andalouse	22
Sole: mousse	120
Squid: black pepper and crispy pork with cashew salad	182
Strawberries: poached in champagne with pannacotta	246
Strawberry and mango lasagna	206
Strawberry: Garigette crème brûlée	166
Sweetbreads: veal with poached lobster tail	142
Sweetbreads: braised veal with morels, truffles, and caramelised apples	74
Sweetbreads: and paupiette of veal flavoured with shallot and garden herbs, Bordelaise potatoes	68
Sweetbreads: with lobster ravioli, braised lambs tongue, crushed peas and marjoram	262
Tartare of sea bass with dill	80
Tartlet of quail and quail eggs with onion confit, summer truffle and smoked bacon, wild mushrooms and a light quail jus	62
Tian of scallop and crab mousse	268
Tronçonettes of lobster, coconut basmati rice, apple, sultanas, and curry sauce	222
Tuna: and sea scallop ceviche, shaved fennel salad, Oscietra caviar with lime dressing	274
Turbot: pan-fried with Jersey Royal potatoes, asparagus, langoustine, horseradish and caviar cream	108
Veal sweetbread with poached lobster tail, chickpea, almond and spice	142
Veal: braised sweetbreads with morels, truffles, and caramelised apples	74
Veal: paupiette flavoured with shallot and garden herbs, Bordelaise potatoes	68
Warm aromatic foie gras, hay sauce	200

ACKNOWLEDGEMENTS

A LA MINE D'ARGENT
Orfévrerie
108, rue du Bac,
75007 Paris
t: +33 145487068
f: +33 145490655
w: www.minedargent.com
e: minedargent@free.fr

YVELINE
Antiquités
4, rue de Furstenberg
75006 Paris
t: +33 143265691
e: antiquitesyveline@yahoo.fr

CONSTANCE MAUPIN
Antiquités, Art de la Table
11, rue du Dr Goujon
75012 Paris
t: +33 143070128

AUX ARMES DE FURSTENBERG
Antiquités, objets de marine
1, rue de Furstenberg
angle 3, rue Jacob
75006 Paris
t: +33 143297951

PETROSSIAN PARIS
traiteur saumon, caviar
18, bld de la Tour Maubourg
75007 Paris
t: +33 144113222
f: +33 144113225
w: www.petrossian.fr

A LA VILLE DE CREMONE
Traiteur italien
76, rue du Bac
75007 Paris
t: +33 145488568

POISSONNERIE DU BAC
69, rue du Bac
75007 Paris
t: +33 145480664

MIS EN DEMEURE
Objets de décoration
27, rue du Cherche Midi
75006 Paris
t: +33 145488335

MAISON DE LA TRUFFE
19, Place de la Madeleine
75008 Paris
t: +33 142655322

AUX FILS DU TEMPS
Tissus anciens
48, rue la Bruyère
75009 Paris
t: +33 145481468
f: +33 145483287
e: auxfilsdutemps@noos.fr